TRUE

AND

FALSE

MAGIC

TRUE
AND
FALSE
MAGIC

A TOOLS WORKBOOK

Phil Stutz

with Elise Loehnen

RANDOM HOUSE

NEW YORK

Random House
An imprint and division of Penguin Random House LLC
1745 Broadway, New York, NY 10019
randomhousebooks.com
penguinrandomhouse.com

A Random House Trade Paperback Original

Published in the United States by Random House, an imprint and division of Penguin Random House LLC, New York.

RANDOM HOUSE and the HOUSE colophon are registered trademarks of Penguin Random House LLC.

Illustration credit Nicholas Blechman

Library of Congress Cataloging-in-Publication Data
Names: Stutz, Phil, author. | Loehnen, Elise, author.
Title: True and false magic / Phil Stutz and Elise Loehnen.
Description: New York, NY : Random House, [2025]
Identifiers: LCCN 2024051272 (print) | LCCN 2024051273 (ebook) |
ISBN 9780593978009 (trade paperback) | ISBN 9780593978016 (ebook)
Subjects: LCSH: Self-actualization (Psychology) | Change (Psychology)
Classification: LCC BF637.S4 S84855 2025 (print) | LCC BF637.S4 (ebook) |
DDC 158.1—dc23/eng/20241218
LC record available at https://lccn.loc.gov/2024051272
LC ebook record available at https://lccn.loc.gov/2024051273

Printed in the United States of America on acid-free paper

randomhousebooks.com

2 4 6 8 9 7 5 3 1

Book design by Mary A. Wirth

The authorized representative in the EU for
product safety and compliance is Penguin Random House Ireland,
Morrison Chambers, 32 Nassau Street, Dublin D02 YH68, Ireland.
https://eu-contact.penguin.ie.

To Barry Michels. You taught me to find magic in the darkest moments.

CONTENTS

INTRODUCTION

I'm not special.

I never thought I'd be a public figure or a bestselling author. In fact, for the first stretch of my life, I didn't even think I was intelligent. I had the perfect parents to perpetuate an ignorance about who I was, because they didn't know either. But oddly, their dismissiveness kept me on track. Left to my own devices, I would have become a writer.

Instead, I became a psychiatrist. My parents wanted me to be a doctor, and I didn't want to be persona non grata in my family, so I obliged. My father wanted me to become a pediatrician, because he had lost a child—my younger brother died of a rare kidney cancer when he was three and I was nine. Psychiatry was low on the totem pole in their estimation, and I was conflicted about it, because in my family, you weren't supposed to choose your life based on what you wanted or how you felt. But I decided to choose myself. I loved working with people, but right from the beginning, I knew something was missing. I quickly discovered that the go-to position in treating psychiatric patients was a combination of a psychotherapy model, which I didn't believe in at all, and medications, which sometimes worked well and other times made things worse. What struck me the most was that psychiatry was supposed to be the medical discipline that was the most human—but to my disappointment, treating psych patients at the time didn't emphasize the humanity of a patient at all. It was all about diagnostic codes.

For all these reasons, I was never a typical psychiatrist. I tried to give people tools that work. I don't think of myself as someone who created something spectacular, but I do think that I have become a very good teacher.

Some of my patients tell me that I can do things for them that they think are magic. In this book, I'm going to teach you how to do this work with yourself. I will give you a process, a protocol, to create real magic. Not fake magic, but real magic.

I first learned about what I've come to call the three domains (Uncertainty, Pain, and the Need for Constant Work) and the demands you must meet to engage with them in my early life, even though I didn't have the words for them then.

I grew up in the Bronx, with two parents who were not happy—though they were unhappy in different ways. Neither of my parents was functional. My father was the youngest of fourteen children—he and his older half brother were the only boys, and he had a sea of sisters. Most of my family got out of Europe before the Holocaust, but I believe four aunts died.

I don't know if factors from his early childhood influenced his behavior, but my father was out there. On Sunday mornings, I'd get up at nine o'clock to play basketball and he would already have read every fucking newspaper, including four from New York, some from the West Coast, and dispatches from Europe. He wanted to master information so that he could predict the future.

When I came home from school, he would be in his chair and insist that I sit at his feet, not to demean me, but because he was a fanatic. He had all these theories and predictions about the world— they held me in their thrall tremendously, even though they were wrong. As I grew up, my father's illusions about the world proved unsustainable. There was too much evidence in the other direction. Because his predictions failed, he had nothing that made him feel good about himself, or that made him feel he deserved to be on earth. More than anything else, he didn't understand the necessity of work to make his life feel meaningful. The Devil sold my father on a very subtle form of getting "over" without meeting God: He thought there were substitutes to spiritual work.

My father couldn't stand being vulnerable to anything—he was very smart, and he hoped that his intellect would be enough. He had a Marxist worldview that everything was predetermined, that everything could be analyzed and predicted, and that people and groups of people—the police, doctors, etc.—could self-regulate in the right political system.

My father taught me a lot about the domain of Uncertainty, which we will address in this book. He was unwilling to accept uncertainty and thought he could engineer his life against it.

My mother, on the other hand, was not engaged with the world—she could shut it out, and that was her preference. On a beautiful sunny day in the tenements of the Bronx, when every kid and every adult would be out in the street, she would lock herself inside and read a book. That was heaven to her.

My mother's father was a psychopath. He abandoned them in 1933—my grandmother and two young girls—with no money. My mom was about twelve when this happened. A day after he left, my grandmother got a notice that her checks weren't clearing. She went down to the bank, the banker pulled out all the papers, and she discovered that my grandfather had tricked her into signing a note. He had taken everything and moved to Florida.

My mom was a bookworm and a genius, but she was never happy. Her son, my younger brother, died at the age of three, which was devastating—but she hadn't been happy even before that. She was inconsolable—and her grief gave her even more reason to stay in the Maze (see p. 67). Her whole life was about feeling injured and getting revenge. She was unwilling to move forward by dealing with the domain of Pain.

Meanwhile, I learned about the domain of Constant Work through my health, because cognitively, I haven't always needed to work hard. In medical school at NYU, my classmates would get pissed at me and ask if I had found a way to cheat. I was one of only six students out of 120 who passed the physiology test—if you failed this test, you had to take the entire term over—even though I went out clubbing most nights.

Early in my life, I didn't know that working with people's minds was my mission or that I was good at it. The only thing I knew was that I wanted to make money and heal myself. And God laughed and said, *I will give you double the money and half the health.* I didn't understand it then, but my long struggles with poor health were important. All of these guys who became big shots ended up putting money and power above everything else. But my Parkinson's disease made so many things impossible, and therefore my life possible. For example, I couldn't be a surgeon, and I couldn't get up at five o'clock in the morning; it would have been a disaster. So I became a psychiatrist. My physical limitations protected me. And because I didn't give up, I had to develop an abnormal will. Despite having Parkinson's and being in my late seventies now, I have no interest in retiring. I feel as though the steps I went through in my life, which I admit were unusual, were engineered by some force to match my life experiences perfectly with my mission.

WHEN I WAS six years old, I lived in Manhattan on the same block as my friend Sharon, whose mother, Lenore, was my mom's best friend. One day, my mother and Lenore drove to the Bronx to see their mothers, who conveniently lived in the same building. Back then, when it was a nice day, everyone would be out on the street, so my mom told me to stay outside while she went upstairs to visit her mom. I waited outside for twenty minutes or so until Lenore and my mother came downstairs. They started walking toward the car and I followed them, when out of nowhere a little kid, maybe nine years old, jumped in front of me, as though he needed to protect my mom and Lenore from me. All I had to do was say, "Hey, that's my mother." But a force I couldn't control rose up within me, and I refused to identify myself, which immediately started a fight between us. Eventually, I broke down and told this other kid who I was; otherwise, he would have kicked my ass.

On our way back to Manhattan, I kept thinking about this

strange situation, wondering why I had acted that way, and why I had refused to tell this kid who I was. That was the first time I became aware that something in me didn't add up. I didn't know more than that, just that something was wrong. That's as far as I got.

I encountered this force again in my childhood in a way that left an indelible mark on me. It wasn't quite the same as the first experience, but I knew it was the same force. My apartment was near the nursery school I went to, so I'd usually walk home after. But one day, my parents said, "David Goldwater is having a birthday party, and you can go right there from school. You don't have to go home. And not only that, but you can also go there on the school bus." I had never done this before. I was thinking, *This is too good to be true. This can't possibly happen.* When we got to the right stop, the driver opened the bus door, and I panicked. I thought, *There's no way I can get down those stairs.* Finally, my classmates dragged me down, and I had a good time at the party. But the point is that I had felt something incredibly negative, something adamant about destroying all of my hope. As a child, I couldn't even try to define this counterforce, but in a way, its presence didn't surprise me. I knew and felt that it was very real.

In my teens, we lived in one of those post-war faceless brick apartment buildings. We had two pimps as neighbors: Leroy and "the Snake." And luckily, or unluckily, they really liked us. Leroy, in particular, couldn't stop talking and loved talking to me and my sidekick, Seymour, who was a fantastic character. They knew I planned to become a shrink, so Leroy wanted to teach me some things about human psychology and human interaction—but mostly, he was grandiose, and just wanted someone to listen to his bullshit. Over time, as he opened up to me, what he told me did change my life— because he was the Devil, or Part X, embodied. Leroy and the Snake would run as many as a dozen women every night—they would drive around in cars and make sure these women were doing their business.

One day, I asked Leroy, carefully, "How do you manage so many people?"

He said, "It starts the first moment I meet them. Most of them are from out of town. My job is to break down their egos completely and make them feel like they can't live without me. I never have sex with them. I never give them any independent power. I tally the money every night and keep precise accounting. Once in a while, I give them something nice, like a jacket or new dress. That lasts about three or four months, and then I need to do it again. The whole gig is to keep them dependent on me so they don't think they can live without me."

I found this information shocking, but I could see that it was true. Leroy told me that he could turn anyone, man or woman, into an equivalent of these prostitutes. He taught me the power human beings can have over others without doing very much—all he had to do was trigger a woman's Part X.

These were my first encounters with Part X, an entity that I've written about extensively in the first two books I co-authored with Barry Michels: *The Tools* and *Coming Alive.* We will talk about Part X in this book as it is one of our primary companions. I didn't know what I was contending with early in my life, but now I understand this counterforce to the Life Force, which I'll explain soon.

I went to Stuyvesant High School, which I fucking hated because the desks were drilled to the floor. The entire place was crumbling; it was all boys, and it was a long subway ride, so I didn't have many friends. Being on the basketball team might have been a source of friendships for me, but the coach wouldn't put me on the team. I played on another team instead.

The basketball coach at Stuyvesant, the one who wouldn't put me on the team, was a guy named Mr. Cavallaro, who wore his socks up to his knees. There was this kid named Charlie Scott who rode the bench—he went on to become a three-time NBA All Star. Next to him on the bench was Barry Leibowitz, who also later played pro ball for many years. Mr. Cavallaro didn't perceive their abilities, which was nuts—he didn't know what he was dealing with.

I started college when I was sixteen years old—it was somehow easier to get on the basketball team in college as a sixteen-year-old than it had been in high school. It was there that I developed my first tool, although I didn't call it a tool then. The basketball coach hated me, really hated me. He would get angry at me, and then I would get tense and defiant. There wasn't much of a meeting of the minds. Things changed when I was a senior, mainly because I was the only guy who could handle the ball.

When my coach was bearing down on me, I got the idea to use a mantra, though I didn't know that word at the time. I would silently say *heart* to connect to my courage, and I would repeat it over and over again. That word would shut everything out—I wouldn't care what my coach or anyone in the stands thought about me. Everything would fade away, including my nervousness. It was like hypnotizing myself. I couldn't explain what happened. I didn't know how to articulate it. I had no opinion on it. I was raised in a family where if you voiced anything like that, they would think you had lost your mind. The idea that a tool could change your inner state? That was not something that existed.

After I graduated from the NYU School of Medicine, I went into private practice. This was the 1970s, when the war wasn't over yet and the country was in chaos. I had committed to being in the Navy, but then there was a bombing in Cambodia, and I decided fuck this, I'm not going. But because I had already been inducted, I had to go through this whole rigamarole to reclassify myself as a conscientious objector. As a make good, I had to do five years as a civil servant, so I worked as a prison psychiatrist at Rikers Island.

While people are fascinated by this experience, it was demoralizing. I felt as if I had nothing to offer the patients in my private practice *or* these prisoners, though I came to understand that both patient populations were subject to outside forces, which I eventually called Part X. At times, my private practice patients were crazier: Sometimes powerful people are far more dangerous than convicts.

I never cared what people had done to end up in prison. I only cared whether they would participate going forward in finding a way to control themselves. I didn't have the language at the time for Part X. I would say, "There's something inside you that doesn't want you to live, be happy, or survive. It's working against you, and you must be proactive in dealing with it."

The presence of Part X is pervasive—I felt a commonality between my patients who were inmates and my patients who were not locked up. One of my free patients killed her mother at this time. She was a chronic schizophrenic and heavy drinker who had been pretty well under control. Her mother was also a chronic schizophrenic and a heavy drinker. I told my patient that if she ever drank again, she should call me immediately, because she could become psychotic. I got home one day and there were all these crazy messages on my answering machine. An hour later, I heard from a cop who asked me if she was my patient, because she had just killed her mother. She had called me and then not put the phone down—the entire event was recorded on my answering machine. I spent a day and a half in court. She only did five weeks in jail because they didn't know how to deal with a schizophrenic.

In that same six-week period, another patient jumped out of a six-story window on Central Park South and lived—the last time I saw him, he was in a cast up to his eyeballs. Another patient was not so lucky. She had gotten a new apartment and wanted to buy a sofa instead of therapy. I told her that was fine, but that she had better not stop seeing me, so I compromised that she could come every other week. Our first week off in between sessions, she took pills, though she immediately realized she didn't want to die. She walked herself to Metropolitan Hospital for help and then died anyway. The point is, throughout my career, whether I'm working with prisoners, normal citizens, or celebrities, I've also been working with invisible forces, forces that are much more powerful than you might think.

I didn't start formally developing the Tools technique until the 1980s, in part because I came to hate what I refer to as "loose talk." Back in the day, someone would go to a psychoanalyst, and they would talk for a while, or even for a few years, and it didn't matter. The sessions would achieve nothing. As I was being trained, I saw this happen in front of my face. To me, it's loose talk if the shrink says or implies, "Now you can change," when they haven't given the patient anything practical. As a psychiatrist, I couldn't figure out how somebody could change through only talking and thinking.

It also drove me nuts that people were spending so much money on therapy. I'm a mercenary—I love money—but I couldn't stand what I witnessed. It was like thirty plumbers going into a building, and when they leave, there's shit all over the floor. It offended me. It wasn't the patients' fault; it was happening because they were subject to loose talk from therapists, which basically amounted to assumptions of change that didn't have to be borne out. These assumptions were often supported with nothing more than the idea that back in the day, "Freud said it." That was supposed to be enough. To this day, therapists continue to benefit from the natural authority of being the therapist, because they function as a working part of some conceptual entity that's founded on nothing.

The old psychoanalytic model is based on theoretical information that can't be proven. This model relies on telling people that the source of their problems is historical or biochemical and that there's a specific cause. It almost works backwards, in that whatever conclusion they come to, they then assume *a priori* that it explains the behavior, which if you think about it logically is ridiculous. Let's say that you are anxious. A psychotherapist might say that your anxiety comes on because your father used to beat the shit out of you. They latch on to what they decide is the cause and then use it as a generative stem to explain every misfiring in your life. They might be right, but they certainly can't prove it. For me, doing this felt like a psychoanalytic jerk-off: Patients would leave these sessions with *nothing.* I couldn't accept it.

It is very difficult to go from the theoretical to a place where you are affecting a human being, to take something you learn intellectually and make it into something that you can feel. This is the brilliance of the tools: They bridge thinking and feeling in a single action. In my process, I don't give my clients ease. I tell them the truth within reason. They come back, desperate for more of the truth. And desperate for tools that work. I give my clients homework and expect them to put the tools to use in their lives. The tools are not a theoretical model; they are practical strategies which must be used, not simply thought about.

You might be asking what the difference is between going to the shrink, having that professional elucidate or tell you your problem, and identifying a symptom and using a tool to make you feel a bit better. Maybe it sounds like a similar process. But it's not. This book isn't about symptom amelioration; it's about getting you in motion, really into motion, in your life.

This is a training program where everyone ends up with the same skills. My first book, *The Tools,* was about addressing a symptom: You have a symptom; we have a tool that will make the symptom go away, or at least attenuate it. That's good, but it's not good enough. This is a global training program. It's the same program for everybody. This doesn't obviate that everybody has an individualistic life, and that the superficial details of someone's life are completely different from someone else's. But it does insist that there are universal ways to engage with higher forces and move forward.

DID YOU EVER talk to someone and find there's so much agreement, you can skip the phase where you align your worldviews? Sometimes that happens with friends. It's an instinctual connection, and I had it from the first second with Rudolf Steiner, who died more than twelve years before I was born. He has been one of my primary teachers, someone whose work I intuitively understand. Everything he has written or said feels like something I already knew but had not yet realized.

Rudolf Steiner said that the basis of human behavior is simple: The default position is fear and laziness. This is why it's so hard for people to change. I've come to believe that he's right, and that these two qualities define core avoidance. He also wrote about how advanced humans have three different brains: the Willing Brain, the Feeling Brain, and the Thinking Brain. I've come to understand that these capacities are closely aligned with the three domains I outline in this book. To contend with the three domains, you must (re)develop the capacity to *will, feel,* and *think.*

Because I write and talk about the Shadow and Part X (see p. 33), people think I'm a Jungian, but I find Carl Jung to be too Teutonic, in that he put too much faith in the power of self-discipline. Whether it's on the Supreme Court, with someone who handles money, or on a basketball team, no human being is completely self-regulated. An honest person isn't afraid to say, *"Have someone watch me and keep me on track,"* because they recognize they might need it. Carl Jung believed that if you put someone in therapy and gave them a bit of orientation, they could come up with their own answers and solutions. Bullshit—nothing is self-regulated.

When it came to developing the tools, I took a lot of patterns from my parents and from my own life, and a lot from my patients. When I work with patients, I want them to focus on themselves and finding their way forward—not to worry about the meaning of every lesson or the order of the universe. Their experiences and insights give me directions, but creating the map is my job.

Speaking of my job, I have been a psychiatrist for more than forty years, but only recently have I realized how little I knew about my chosen field. My work was good, I was able to help a lot of people, but there was a level of understanding I had never reached. My punishment was to be known as "the psychiatrist to the stars." This workbook that you're holding is a gesture toward my deeper understanding of the universe and how it functions to co-create with us when we're willing to engage with the three unavoidable realities of life: pain, uncertainty, and the need for constant work.

I believe that the tools are more important than ever because *creativity is the adversary of evil.* In some ways, this is the only thing you need to understand. Our ability to approach the changes in our world relies on how we deal with evil.

We all feel that something has changed. So many of us are deeply unsatisfied. On a global basis, wars are sprouting.

In the recent past, institutions gave us some sense of safety, even a sense that our fate might be predictable. But in the era of COVID, it feels as though we can't continue to rely on the same institutions as we have for the last fifty, one hundred, or two hundred years. Anxiety and depression are off the charts. But people don't understand that there's something even deeper and more significant that's destroying our institutions, from the Supreme Court to Congress to public education.

There's a force in the universe, which I call Part X, that does not want us to know who we are or what we are capable of. Part X is a devious force that weakens us and makes it impossible to develop our potential. This force wants to take the free part of the human being—the part that's resourceful, and can recover well, and has a broader consciousness—for its own uses. Part X doesn't want to kill that part of you; it wants to appropriate it. In the old days, they would call it eating someone's soul.

There is a war going on right now. You might think you can ignore it or that it doesn't affect you, but it will work its way out until, sooner or later, everyone is involved. It's a battle for the nature of the human soul. The tools allow anybody and everybody to participate in this battle in a productive way by putting them in touch with higher forces. It might sound stupid to use the model of war, but it's a good model to describe the monumental and powerful effects it will have on all of us. Every metaphorical bullet counts. What makes this book unique is that I'm training people not just for their own personal satisfaction or even their own survival. We are preparing soldiers to do battle for the earth's survival. This is a collective action.

You can't do anything that has any meaning all by yourself. It's impossible. Everything that a person accomplishes that is real, that's not just superficial, requires higher forces. Evolution must be a co-creation with these higher forces. In my experience, the way to activate them is to use the tools on the problems that present themselves in your life. Those problems, however mundane and basic they may seem, are the bridge to get you to use the tools to touch and direct higher forces (see p. 23). These problems become the training ground for you to learn how to work with the universe.

Most people are unable to get what they need out of life because they're either too lazy or too frightened. We will explore these tendencies much more deeply throughout this book, but most of us aren't functioning up to our potential as humans. It's so obvious it's almost a ridiculous thing to say. The reason is also obvious: Everyone wants a free pass. No one likes discomfort. We live in a delusional culture where we're mostly damaging ourselves in our avoidance of the reality of life. Avoidance, or resistance, will never stop reality—but it can stop you from experiencing life.

The universe is constructed in a very specific way, with a very specific purpose. The purpose of the universe is to force humans to evolve. God, or whatever you want to call him, doesn't care about anything else. If the universe were not constructed in this way, the universe would have no meaning at all. Each of the three domains that I outline in this book represents one fact, or one quality of the universe: I think of them as the three faces of God.

We do not live in a meaningless universe—but you are required to harvest the meaning. The deepest part of evolution is that we are forced to create. God created something out of nothing and shared this superpower with us. It isn't a value judgment; it is just a reality. This is a magical fact. Anyone who remembers this while studying or using this book will find a way to proceed, especially if they feel demoralized, or if they've lost a sense of faith. When you look at the effect on a person who is no longer allowed to avoid—when they are forced to meet their karma, or fate, or whatever you want to call it— you will discover real magic, which can only be achieved through creativity. The domains are designed to train one for this process.

Human beings have infinite potential. Now, that's a cheap thing to say because everybody says it, but the point of this process is to give people a pathway that will unleash some of that potential. You must understand that your potential is part of your birthright. God made us with this force, or potential, inside of us—and then set it up so that it must be accessed, not just given. In fact, the dynamic of this process is that the thing that's most important to you is what you'll actively avoid. God sets it up like this for a reason: It's a training program. You get a superpower when you approach whatever you habitually avoid. To achieve this power, you must pass your course of study here on earth. The course of study is bad things always happening, defined by the demands of three domains: Pain, Uncertainty, and the Need for Constant Work.

Your karma, or mission, or however you want to put it, is placed right in your face—but you must push into and through these three domains. You must push to enter the moving world.

HOW TO USE THIS BOOK

Throughout my career, I have helped people solve problems. That's nice and all, but that's not what this book is about. At first, giving people something to use against panic, heartbreak, obsessive thoughts, impulsivity, and more was enough, until I realized that I was just calming symptoms. My patients needed something more potent. As my patients found faith, freely chosen, their lives and their sense of reality started to move forward.

This book is a training program, not just symptom alleviation. You go to the doctor when you have a symptom—you use a medicine, in this case a tool, and you feel better. The shrinks call that euthymia, which translates to a balance of emotions or a state of internal calm. You can begin with that type of healing to get started, but what we're doing in this book goes way beyond that. A training program forces you to be regimented—and often people don't like that. But the training program in this book will give you access to the strongest force in the universe, the Life Force (see p. 9).

I call the Life Force a directional indicator: It is a mysterious living connection with something that is indefinable on the one hand, but on the other hand, it's like you can smell the next step. This book will not only give you a sense of direction, it's a guide to an actual destination. Your Life Force is a guide into the future on the one hand, while connecting you to the future on the other. The Life Force is a real thing.

In sports, watching the game is not the same as playing the game. You must put yourself on the field. In the same way, you get to the destination in this book not just through reading and understanding, but through participation, through your feelings and intuition. Using this book, though it's full of words, should not be merely a cognitive or intellectual process. It's not a book of rules; it outlines a process that you must not only read but *feel*.

The process in this book is one that you must practice—and the practice should lead you to a felt experience. I'd rather you have two seconds of feeling the power of practice than hours of reading hundreds of pages about it. In this book, grasping ideas and concepts is not the only important thing: What matters just as much is sensation, or *feeling*, and willingness. You don't have to believe me or even buy into what I'm saying—just do this process and see what happens.

The real power to create, and the hidden potential of human beings, is unlimited. This workbook is about getting real magic or power, not fake magic or symbolic power. Your biggest hopes and dreams can come true—but not without accepting that this is difficult. God gave human beings the power to share in his creative powers. You don't have to believe this, but in the following pages, I will give you an experience of it, which is more important than what you believe.

God reveals himself in three domains. Each domain contains some aspect of God, and each domain has its own demand. You can't have access to the powers that God wants everyone to have, and you cannot really experience reality, until you contend with the three domains, the three big unavoidable realities of life. First, I will introduce you more deeply to some key concepts like your Life Force, higher forces, Universe One and Universe Two, and Part X. I will explain why so many people are deluding themselves in a place called the Realm of Illusion and constraining themselves in the Safety Zone. Then, you will enter the three domains around which this book is structured and get to work. While the content of each domain will be different, the intention is the same: to bring each domain to a point, which is called the Y. The first domain is Pain, the second is Uncertainty, and the third is the Need for Constant Work. While I've had to write this book as a linear process—one domain following the next—you cannot unlock the Y until you learn to work these domains simultaneously. They are mutually arising.

The three domains, in combination, unlock real magic, not fake power. Once you learn to move through pain, you will gain the ability to expand; once you develop faith, freely chosen, to contend with uncertainty, you will gain the ability to decide and create; and once you embrace constant work, you will gain the ability to be infinite. The height of this power is the ability to turn nothing into something. That's the function of God. That's the definition of creativity. That's real magic.

God made us so that we can endure the undeniable realities of the three domains, but it's difficult—Part X is always there, whispering in our ears that it's bullshit. That it's impossible. Humans are built to do this, but we're not allowed to do what we are meant to do at 100 percent, because it must be done with complete free will and without prior knowledge of exactly what's going to work. If there were no uncertainty, if we were given a complete set of instructions and assurance of the result, there would be no willpower in it, and no freedom.

There are not a lot of words in this book because working with the tools is not a cognitive process: It's not enough for you to flip through this, read it quickly, or even read it thoroughly. You must use the tools over and over again. You will need to read this book more than once. There are enough tools in this book to keep you busy until you die. To make an impact on this world, you must access higher forces. Until you can feel these powers in your body, you really haven't gotten what you can out of this book.

You don't have to accept what I'm saying; you can still use the tools as if you accept it. Because we're all connected, one or two people using the tools can influence the entire group—and they won't even know they're being influenced. You don't even have to know, or care, if you're influencing them.

Throughout my career, something interesting would happen when I would lead a seminar. There would be one or two people who would say, "This is bullshit." I would tell them that they might be right. I wouldn't try to convince them otherwise. I would convince them to try a tool. They would become the best students because they would have no pretense or belief that they knew what was happening. They didn't bother trying to prove anything; they simply understood that the tools work.

I want you to think of this book like a bomb. It's going to release certain forces in your life, forces that are already there but have not yet been accessed.

There's an invisible structure built into the universe, and the tools are designed to work in harmony with that underlying structure. You can reap tremendous power from doing so; your belief is not required. Let's begin.

TRUE
AND
FALSE
MAGIC

The Frame

I f I had to guess, you've come to this book because you've experienced at least one psychological death—by that, I mean that something has happened to you that you would not have chosen. It could be a real death, the loss of a job or a relationship, or any other change in status that feels catastrophic. That catastrophe breaks the frame.

I want you to imagine the way that you perceive your life as a diorama, like the ones you might see at the Museum of Natural History in New York City. This is how we see the world, where everything outside of the frame is not real. Most of us live a very limited existence inside this frame—we're constricted. This happens because we think we have no other choice.

When we don't understand something intellectually, or it doesn't cohere with our worldview, we kick it out of the diorama so that it no longer exists for us. This gives us a certain sense of control—and to be fair, the good thing about this frame is that it does create order in our lives to a certain degree. But we pay a very large price for this: It's what keeps us living such a tiny life, even if we've succeeded.

It's only when something happens that challenges this framework that we become conscious of its existence. Paradoxically, we experience this event as death. Not a physical death but a shattering of the framework. It feels like death because you believe that living inside

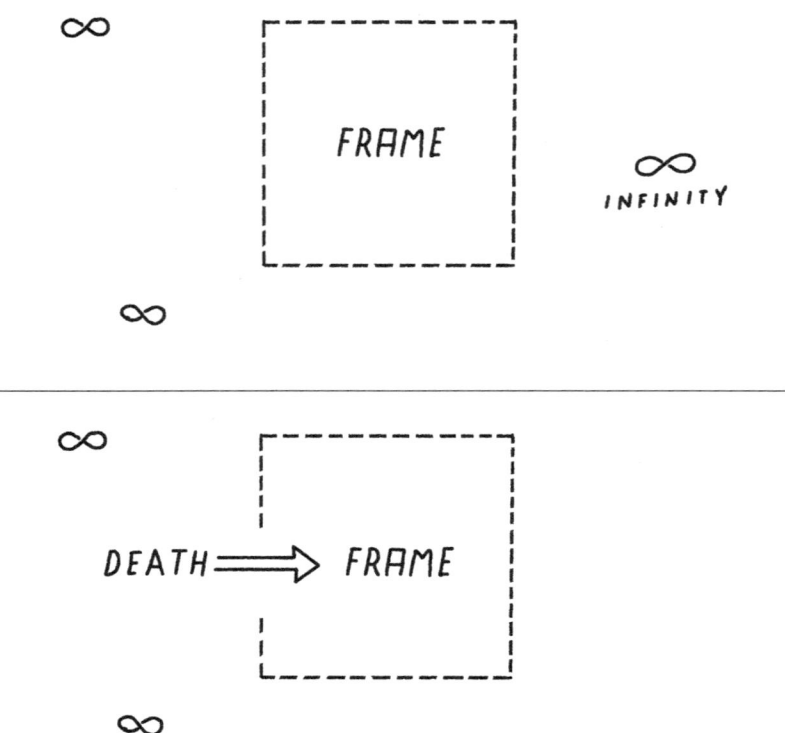

the frame will keep you safe. The death event breaks this frame and demolishes the idea that it will provide existential security. Your belief system is shattered as well, and the whole universe begins to come in through the windows and doors as a tremendous, indefinable, and infinite force that can't be stopped. The universe intrudes and destroys your worldview. Everything looks different. Consciously, we think of these death events as bad, but if you are prepared, you can learn from them and begin to understand what they are: an opportunity to live beyond your frame.

You also come to understand that these punches in the face are unpredictable and also unceasing: They are not going to stop, but you will begin to see them in a completely new way. If you know how to react to these face punchings, they won't ever feel good—but they will feel meaningful. You are feeling the presence of God.

The explosion of the frame that contains your life is a co-venture with God. You need events, or deaths, to shatter the frame, which gives you access to infinite creative potential. We love to judge our lives by the results—a bestselling novel, selling your company, landing a promotion—but God is not interested in that, or in any other material objective. God is a process. In the same way—and very few people understand this—death is not a permanent state but is instead part of a cycle. All of creativity is an endless stream of death and rebirth.

Now, you might think that when the frame explodes, you enter another frame, one that might be bigger. But no, that's not the point—when the frame shatters, you are granted the opportunity to enter the three domains which are the structure of this book. Only after the frame shatters does it become possible to co-create with God or the universe. The frame is the starting block, your introduction to this preexisting creative flow. We will never know where this flow comes from or where it's going, in the same way that the universe is literally made from the ability to create something out of nothing. This same force allows you to create something out of nothing. You can't really explain or understand this—it will break your brain. It just is.

Once you're in this energy of creation, you will come in and out of it. This is natural, since it would be impossible to stay in a flow of creativity constantly—and it's natural to feel resistance. When you stand on the banks of this river and cling to the edge, you're avoiding engaging with the domains. Hopefully this workbook convinces you to get back in the flow. The universe is an endless curlicue of creative expansion that is always available to us and can be entered infinitely: All we're trying to do here is put this energy on our team, to harness it and access it.

You will unlock a new kind of energy I call "dual consciousness," which represents the solution to the paradox of being human. It means you can pursue your personal goals and desires and at the same time contribute to the well-being of the collective. The fact that you can be in these two states simultaneously is the reason we call it dual consciousness.

The topic of avoidance will come up frequently in this workbook. The three domains you're avoiding are proxies for God: They're initiatory. They are coexistent—not separate from one another even though I'm giving them to you as three domains. God knows what to present you with to force your own evolution, which is why it doesn't really matter which domain you focus on: They all lead to the same place. They all lead to the Y.

PART I

CHAPTER 1

The Life Force

Meet Your Life Force

Throughout my career, I would often find myself confronted with a certain type of patient. Usually, it would be a middle-aged guy who had gone to a school like Harvard.

He'd say something like, "I can't control my temper, my wife says I'm an addict, I gamble, I just lost $92,000 in Las Vegas, I'm miserable," etc. And then he would say, "If only I knew why I was here. If I only knew my mission, I'd be motivated and able to do all these things that are difficult for me. But I feel hopeless, because I don't know how to find out what my mission is."

First, I would tell him that he's an ungrateful baby.

Now, I could look at him—or a patient who may appear to be even more depressed—on a purely symptomatic basis and come up with a diagnosis. But this wouldn't enhance my relationship with him. If I believe everything has a cure, then people become an impersonal, scientific, logical problem to solve. And diagnosing becomes a dry, soulless, and ultimately less effective way to deal with life.

Instead, I would then explain to him that I can't tell him his mission, and that the source of knowledge about his life purpose isn't in his head. Your head can't know it.

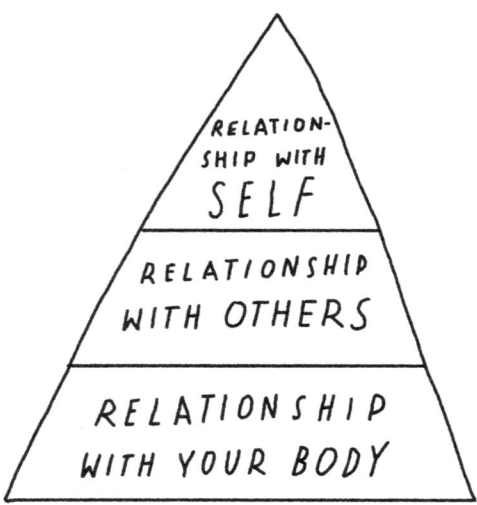

"Your Life Force," I would say, "is the part that's going to point you toward your mission in life and why you're here. It's not something you think; you have to feel it."

And then he'd say, "Why can't you just tell me what it is?"

"I can't tell you because I don't know. Everyone has to discover this for themselves. The discovery of this is not a singular conclusion; it's a process."

"Well, that's very nice, but I have to start somewhere."

"Start with yourself. This may seem far-fetched, but every human being has some energy inside them, some potential that will help them find their ultimate goal. But you can't go right to the macro goal. It's impossible. You can try, but you'd be kidding yourself."

During a conversation like this, a typical shrink might ask, "What inspires you, what turns you on, what makes you think you know who you are? Because that will lead you out of this morass." But I know this is bullshit. You can't think yourself to a conclusion.

So instead, I would say, "Even though consciously you don't have an idea of who you are or what would make your life meaningful, there's a part of every human being that holds their potential. If they follow the rules, every person can find their way to this energy that everybody has, which has tremendous power. But you must start at the bottom. There's a generic approach to the Life Force. You must function as if you have faith in that, even though you might not. God made every human being with an energy unique to that individual. The problem is that in our culture, we always think about the final, macro, outer expression of that. But you only get this by going through the discipline of connecting to the universal Life Force. You may not find it as exciting or as inspiring as you imagine, but the power starts at the bottom."

When I know he's willing, I offer the following: "You're going to start by getting off your ass, turning the TV off, and walking around the block."

This may sound like a pale response to something like depression, which could take someone's life. And this is true. But people must start by getting in touch with their Life Force, which requires building a relationship with its three pyramidal tiers: You must build your relationship with your body, your relationship with other people, and your relationship with yourself. You start with the body. This never fails to bring someone's Life Force up a notch.

Like so many others, this patient's Life Force is trapped in entropy. He is not alone or unusual. There's a generic, predictable set of rules and a dynamic to connect you to your Life Force, whether you like it or not. Doing this has nothing to do with your job or other facts of your life. It only concerns the three tiers of relationship: The more you work the relational pyramid, the stronger your Life Force will become.

The Qualities of the Life Force

Have you ever met someone with a high Life Force who didn't know what to do with their life? Probably not. We tend to assign this quality of having your shit together to "a healthy ego," but that's wrong. This person is actually in touch with their Life Force. The Life Force is something that most people don't understand, a force which exists and can't be proven. It just is.

The Life Force is a profound and mysterious power responsible for intuition, creativity, identity, and recovery. By connecting with it, you'll develop stronger instincts, though faith will be key to this transition. Opportunities to connect to the Life Force are always present, and it's never too late to build that relationship. This connection must be nurtured on three levels: with your body, others, and yourself.

The Life Force is a cognitive organ: It's a part of you, and you can relate to it. The relationships to your body, other people, and yourself weave together to form the Life Force in its most primal form. When you do this, the wisdom of *What should I do next—do I want to be a doctor?* tends to come, too.

The key to the Life Force is recuperation and recovery—in fact, you won't really feel your Life Force until you break the Frame (see p. 3) by experiencing a crisis, or psychological death, and recover. Death and rebirth itself is a cosmic pattern that cannot be violated. Understanding this completely changes the meaning of failure and gives you a new definition of flow, which is the ability to subsume two opposite things at the same time.

The Life Force is the creative heart of the universe and every individual, a gift from God that interweaves energies and relationships. It embodies your unrealized potential and compels action toward discovering your purpose. To connect with it, you must work continuously on all three levels. As these connections strengthen, so does your sense of self and motivation. The Life Force is both eternal and present, providing intuition and wisdom beyond intellect. It allows you to create yourself anew, offering rebirth and renewal in an endless cycle of creation.

The Life Force holds the past, present, and future and exists within every human being. It is a humble, disciplined, and self-renewing power that enables you to align with reality, fight against destructive forces, and embrace creativity as an antidote to evil. Through it, you can achieve what once seemed impossible. The Life Force is deeply connected to everything, constantly creating something from nothing and helping you navigate the future—not by seeing it, but by feeling it.

You don't have to believe this for it to work, but I can promise you that you're not going to know anything until you get in touch with your Life Force. Your Life Force will give you an answer, but it won't be a printout. You'll still need to take action in the face of no proof. But this is where the process begins.

Patient Story: Losing Everything

Here's a story that offers an extreme example of the power of the Life Force. A guy walked into my office who historically had run huge companies and led massive teams. He had made millions, maybe even billions, of dollars. When he came to me, his business was failing and his life was a mess: He was cheating on his wife, gambling, using drugs almost daily. And he was deeply cynical.

The problem wasn't just that he had lost money. He had lost his identity, and he had no idea what to do. As is typical of people in that situation, he blamed his business failure and the chaos in his life on the world and didn't want to take any responsibility for it himself.

I told him that the Life Force is real and he could have access to it, and he reacted as the average person does. He resisted.

I told him, "I can't prove it until you do what I say. But I guarantee you if you do what I say, you will feel something."

I didn't think he would agree. But to my surprise, and I think out of desperation, he said, "Okay, I'll try what you're asking me to do. I'm going to force myself to have faith in this."

I said, "Okay, but there's one more thing. You have to measure your faith in the smallest possible increments—there's a tool to do this. It's a relational pyramid. It has to do with how you find and activate your Life Force. You must start at the very bottom. Once you do that—even on the smallest level—it will affect everybody around you."

As with everyone, he started with his relationship with his body. He went to the doctor, he started to eat properly, and he started to exercise. I wasn't asking much of him, since these are things he should have been doing anyway. But once he saw that these small changes were part of a larger structure, he started to shift out of seeing this as a way to get out from under a depression that might cause him to kill himself, to seeing this relational pyramid as something he would work on for the rest of his life.

He began to walk, because that was all he could do. A month later, all of a sudden, he had the energy to go to the gym and work out and get back on a bike. His diet improved. He started to look at his physical body as a magical vessel, a foundation from which every other good thing could be accessed. Two surprising things happened: He liked it much more than he'd expected, and he felt a real sense of accomplishment.

Next, he began to regain his sense of leadership, and with that came a little bit of confidence. All of this was triggered by walking around the block and riding his bike. There was something beautiful about this person coming to see that there was no near-term solution to his problems. There was no way for him to return to his previous status, but he had something more valuable, something that could never be taken from him, which was a new understanding of himself.

The other interesting thing that happened almost immediately was that his children became much more attached to him, and much more interested in spending time with him. This opened up the second tier of the relational pyramid—working on your relationship with other people. This was all just from getting on his bicycle. There's no excuse for a person not to work on their relationship with their own body like this. If you do it and it doesn't improve your life, I'll give you a refund on this book. It can't *not* work, which is the beauty of it.

Exercise: Strengthen Your Life Force

You are going to start this process in what I call the World of Small Things. If you can commit to doing something, even if you don't know what that "something" is, it changes your relationship to the person who is guiding you through the process, whether that's your shrink, yourself, or this book in your hands. That commitment changes the entire environment and will give you the first inkling of hope. Start small: If you can't run a mile, run two blocks. Then two additional blocks. In five days, you're running a mile, proving to yourself that it's possible.

You need to strengthen your Life Force in order to do big things with your life—but you will need to start to process these big things through little things and small actions. Let's say that you're eighteen years old and you want to leave home and travel across Europe for the summer. That's a big thing for an eighteen-year-old, and there's not much you can "do" about it when you're at home. But you can do little things to prime yourself: You can read magazine articles and travel guides. You can do research. Those are small things, but they're connected to something big. This infrastructure is the World of Small Things. You need to strengthen your Life Force on all levels— your relationship to your body, your relationship to other people, your relationship to yourself—and we do this through small actions. These actions will underwrite all the things you'd like to do.

RELATIONSHIP WITH BODY: Start in the World of Small Things with achievements that you can track and keep. The smaller and more consistent the effort, the closer you can get to your Life Force. Here's an example of what you can do: Walk for five minutes a day, adding one minute a day until you're walking for thirty minutes every morning. Set an alarm to get in bed ten minutes earlier every night until you've added one to two hours. Schedule that physical that you've put off for five years.

EXERCISE: Make a list of changes you know you need to make, with incremental shifts plotted out, until you reach your goals. Remember, you are creating something out of nothing.

LIST OF CHANGES TO MAKE

List of incremental shifts, i.e. exercise 30 minutes a day might involve starting with 5 minutes and adding 5 minutes every day.
Did you do this?   Y/N

_____

_____

_____

_____

_____

_____

_____

RELATIONSHIP WITH OTHERS: If you need to rebuild your relationship with a parent or a child, call them. Ask someone to have lunch
with you. Go through your phone and respond to texts from last
week or last month. These can't be superficial efforts: You must create
real relationships with real substance. It is impossible to find your
Life Force if you are completely isolated. It is important to feel yourself as part of a unity, as nothing of value is ever created alone.

Very few people think about relationships in these terms. The
Life Force likes every little thing that you do that causes you to reach
out to another person, maintain that relationship, and become more
interested in their life for a bit than your own. The Life Force lives
more intensely if you place it on this level, because everything important in life involves relationship. When it comes to relating to
another person, it's not just about doing your homework or being

disciplined: You're dealing with something that's alive. A relationship is a real thing. Other people can help us, or we can help them, at a profound level. Every time you reach out to another person, if you're consistent with it, you're creating a force. This isn't about averting loneliness; you are trying to create something real, with real substance. The smaller and the more consistent the effort is, the closer you're going to get to the Life Force. The Life Force doesn't care about the size of your victories; it cares about who you are as a human being. Work the relationship pyramid in small, attainable ways.

EXERCISE: Make a list of changes you know you need to make, with incremental shifts plotted out, until you reach your goals. Remember, you are creating something out of nothing.

LIST OF CHANGES TO MAKE

List of incremental shifts, i.e. deepening your relationship with your mother might involve starting with sending a text every week, to calling every Sunday for an hour.

Did you do this?   Y/N

_____

_____

_____

_____

_____

_____

_____

RELATIONSHIP WITH YOURSELF: As the Oracle of Delphi proclaimed, *know thyself*. This level of the pyramid requires complete honesty: The stupidest thing you can do is lie to yourself. Know what you really want, what you really like. Are you creatively stifled? Are you feeling unloved? Get off your ass and find a pencil. Make a pact to write or create every day, again in five- or ten-minute increments. Invest in something for yourself, or take yourself out to dinner and a movie. The Life Force is a gift from God. You can only become aware of this gift if you're willing to go through the initiation, which is each domain's demand. There is a fake Life Force that does not demand uncomfortable honesty or connection, but it is a trick. This fake Life Force suggests that connecting to the real Life Force will be easy, but it isn't connected to anything except your own ego.

EXERCISE: Make a list of changes you know you need to make, with incremental shifts plotted out, until you reach your goals. Remember, you are creating something out of nothing.

LIST OF CHANGES TO MAKE

List of incremental shifts, i.e. if writing a screenplay is your dream, begin by writing five minutes a day and build up from there.
Did you do this?   Y/N

_____

_____

_____

_____

_____

The combination of all of these relationships is magical. This is *not* a checklist; this is a process that you need to begin to engage with: The *work* you need to do on your Life Force is never-ending.

The Tents

If you track your path through life, there are moments as you move forward where you fuck up, or your discipline breaks down, and you're off the path. This happens to everyone—there's no shame in it—but you have to then choose to get back on the path. The truth is made at this moment, which is why I call it the "moment of truth." The moment of truth has nothing to do with how well you've done in your life. It is choosing to go back inside the channel where you were functioning in a healthy way. The moment of truth is when you ask yourself, *Who am I really? Am I really at ease? Am I someone who just wants cheap thrills in this stylized version of the world?* The moment of truth is when your free will comes into play and you must choose to change by saying to yourself, *Do I believe in this enough to get myself back on the path, or do I consciously choose to give up?*

Most of the decision to go back inside your life has to do with discipline, and having a healthy attitude toward life, spirituality, and identity. In this view, meaning must be the most important thing: If you go off the track and you don't correct it in the right way, your life will mean nothing. Meaning is in the curlicues of the Life Force, where the ultimate conquest is conquering these little deaths.

So every time you hit a moment of truth, you make the decision

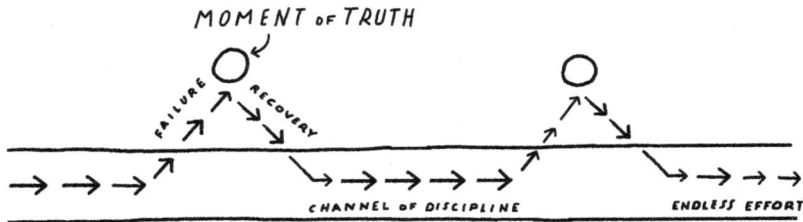

THE TENTS

to get back inside your life and back on the path. And you do this for your entire life. A healthy person has accepted this, and accepted the need for constant work. People make the mistake of assuming people who appear to be very committed and very intelligent are doing "the best." But it's not that simple. Rudolf Steiner says this, and I've found it 100 percent to be true, but it's the person who has failed a lot of times and had to make the decision to get back to life and back on the path, the person who has had a conceptual death experience— who is addicted to drugs, for example, and relapses and gets clean again and again—who is actually stronger and healthier than the person who is merely intelligent. The real definition of death is that it's a prelude to more life. If you look from afar at the trajectory of a person who is making positive decisions to get back on the path of their life, you will see a series of tents. This is the real picture of the Life Force in action.

Nonlinear Growth

I want you to recall the frame and how it shatters—and how God continues to introduce symbolic deaths (see p. 77). With these deaths, whether it's an illness, a loss, or a failure, your ego has to die. This might sound terrible, but feel into it: Instinctively, there's some part of you that recognizes that there is something out there for you that you need—but to accomplish it, your ego needs to be shattered because this thing is too big for your ego to contain. This is a positive thing even though it's painful. The Life Force counters these deaths.

Recovery or rebirth from this type of death does not feel resolvable unless you have access to the Life Force to make this possible. The Life Force is cyclical; it's like a plant. At the beginning of each curlicue of plant, there's a death that liberates certain parts of the personality that aren't ego-driven. You don't think of a plant as ego-driven, but you certainly can think of a plant as living beyond plant trauma. The plant grows in a nonlinear, forward trajectory—it's a spiral. When you think about this in the context of your life, imagine it as a spiral where you're revisiting experiences in your life from

NON-LINEAR GROWTH

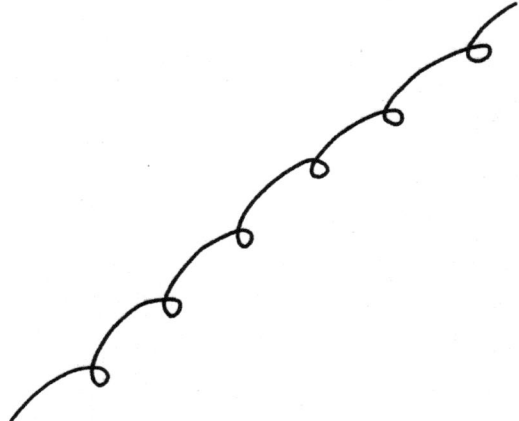

a more evolved or higher level. As we move through life, we have to come back through situations and see them from a different angle. Not only is the Life Force an antidote to ego death and failure, but the curlicues indicate that life is not a smooth and straightforward line: You must get pruned or cut back at times for your own health.

Because the signature of the Life Force is unstoppable recovery, it gives you the power to use the forces of the present to transcend whatever negative stuff feels insoluble. If life were a straight line of growth, you would think you were God and life would be horrible and all evolution would halt. You need these glitches, or prunings, to teach you how to connect to the Life Force in a sober way. Life is an uninterrupted cycle of unstoppability, but to get this superpower, you also need to acknowledge your inability to find or connect to that power without the antecedent failure.

We think we want to move from point A to point B without re-sistance, but it's essential that you feel something impinging on you and impeding your ability to grow. The plant is an important meta-phor for another reason as well, as its nonlinear growth represents the slow revelation of potential. Rudolf Steiner puts it that every flower that blooms, every tree that lives and expands, is not limited to a diorama of three-dimensional space. Part X does not want you to realize this because, logically, you will try to live into it. If you could really feel this space of freedom, nothing could stop you. Steiner calls it the "theory of space." When you're in the first level of life, plant life, the seed doesn't just have the flower in it—it contains the entire world. Only humans can reach the unrealized potential of this world, so long as they're not tethered to a rigid, three-dimensional perception.

The unfolding of the Life Force, which comes with the realization of the importance of creating your own path, is not a neat or tidy process. It's something that hits you when it hits you. Part X (see p. 29) will do whatever it can to re-limit you to a three-dimensional diorama with clear outlines.

CHAPTER 2

Higher Forces

Co-Creating with Higher Forces

The tools in this book are simple, but they are not final solutions: You won't heal a broken heart or achieve financial success by using a tool one time. The tools aren't for curing symptoms, though they might turn the volume down. They are really for touching higher forces. It's only through working with the tools enough that you unlock this special power. Nothing can ever be created by a human being that is valuable, real, lasting, and meaningful unless it is co-created with higher forces. Higher forces are an undifferentiated, essentially indescribable field of energy.

In order for a human being to have any impact in this world, you have to use higher forces; and for higher forces to have an impact in the world, human beings must consciously commit to being their conduit.

You may think that higher forces have to go inside your body, but that's not exactly how it works. The target is not your body; it's a hybrid zone where higher forces and the material world meet—higher forces and humans form a third being, so to speak. We will go deeper into this concept when we get to "The Y" (see p. 117).

If you're going to incarnate here, you have to get into that third

PART 1

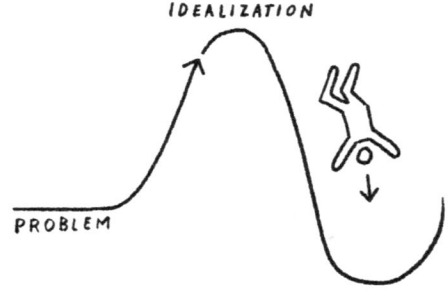

IDEALIZATION

PROBLEM

PART 2

PROBLEM · USE OF TOOLS · HIGHER FORCES

FORCE OF EVOLUTION

being, which is a bridge between the material world and the higher world. You will never be able to do this perfectly or constantly—if you could master it, life would be both over and meaningless. The fact that you must succeed and fail at the same time, that you can't master being a conduit for higher forces, is what makes the universe both whole and incomplete. And yes, this is a paradox: But to cognize anything, to bring anything into the world, means that there must be something missing—wholeness must include the imperfect. The drive for wholeness is not the same thing as wholeness itself—if the universe were whole, there would be no meaning to the creation.

Satisfaction in life is only possible when these two elements are functioning together, combined into this third entity: You're both the bridge and the traveler. It sounds simple, and yet it's remarkably hard.

You don't need to believe in God. You don't even need to believe that there are higher forces participating in reality. In fact, don't try to believe this. Just do exactly what I tell you and see what happens.

Results will not be decided by you. But what is decided by you, every day, every minute, is that you can make a choice to use the tools to access these higher forces—even if you don't believe in them. It's a collective universe, and if you don't know how to use these forces, you're going to fail.

How a Group Creates a Field

There is no such thing as a singular individual human being. Rudolf Steiner would say that even God can't access that degree of possibility.

Our culture is highly individualistic, but on some level, we know that we need one another—to learn and to survive. We also know on some level that nothing actually happens in a silo. Thanks to thermodynamics and quantum physics, we know that in any interaction, you are not the person on the left, nor are you the person on the right: You're neither one; you are the force in between those two vibrations. As physicist Michael Faraday showed us in the 1800s, your body is not a body that can be associated with object A or object B; it's a vibratory energy that's invisible. You might say, "Big deal, he's just another crazy physicist," but it *is* a big deal. We know from Einstein's "spooky action at a distance" theory that electrons have spins on them and they come in pairs. In one pair, you might get a counterclockwise spin, and the other pair might be spinning clockwise. We also know that if you change the spin on the first electron—even at an infinite distance—it will change the spin of the other half of the pair. The electron field is built on the reality that an electron is not an object—it is an energy or force.

We are also not objects. We are vibratory energies in a field. Nothing permanent, and nothing that has real value, could ever be created or supported by one singular person. It's impossible. You cannot work alone. You can co-create with higher forces—invisible unseen powers in the universe—or you can co-create with a group. In fact, a group is capable of drawing down spiritual forces much more strongly and rapidly than someone who is working alone.

Rudolf Steiner said that in the ancient world, there was a much more developed capacity to feel other people. Let's say a thousand people would show up to hear a political figure or priest speak—only the first hundred people could even hear what the guy was saying. They had no way of enhancing sound. But nobody would leave. They would stay, the reason being that everyone's capacity to feel collectively was much stronger then—it wasn't about individual cognition. It's important that we learn how to re-create this sense of feeling, which is difficult because individuality is a much stronger force now—but feeling is the element that holds the meaning. For example, spirituality has to be felt or it isn't real. The mind can use words like "God," and it can create a cognitive concept of God, but this doesn't lend itself to a feeling of God, or to a specific experience. We get that experience through groups and working with higher forces.

Collectively, we need every human soul in the universe to undertake this process to become part of a super force—no exceptions; everyone is part of the whole. No singular person can do anything without a group. The training program in this book is the opposite of the usual use of tools because it's not like being up at the net in tennis, hitting the ball back. If you're at the tennis net, you're in a defensive position, getting the ball out of your side of the court by reacting to an event or a symptom. But this program is the opposite of that. In our view, everybody in the world is on the same court, and the point of the training is that we all have the same goal, which is developing or redeveloping a superpower that was very present in the ancient world. That takes feeling or sensing as a group. In modern times, we've become so cognitive, we've forgotten our instincts and our feelings—we rely solely on our thinking. To get this whole apparatus going again, we have to bring the other two back online.

The only way these superpowers work is when human beings are creating and sharing them simultaneously—it's a singular and collective action, where you serve yourself while serving the whole. The superpower only exists as part of a field. So this is a training program to put everyone in a state of mind where they can connect viscerally, on a feeling level, with everybody else, at least to a degree.

If we go back to the Arthurian Grail myth, and the example of the knight Parsifal, we see that despite doing everything required on the quest, he was barred admittance to the Holy Grail's chamber because he could not come in alone. He had to go and find a partner. Only then could Parsifal and his partner gain admittance to the castle together. We, too, are not supposed to do this work alone.

You cannot create an electron field by yourself. You must create a force that reverberates back and forth with other people.

At my workshops, people come up to me and want to know specific answers—people think I know the answers!—but if you believe in something that has to be A or has to be B, it will be impossible to relate with any kind of depth to another human being, because human beings don't work like that. Our philosophical model has to include two things. Number one, it has to have something for the individual, but not something material, because that won't help them. It can't be just an idea either, but it has to be some kind of procedure or protocol. A philosophy sucks and doesn't truly exist unless it ends in action. Number two, the arbiter of reality can't be the mind—you must be able to sense what the whole needs from you. You will feel an indescribable joy that emerges through you in a way that you cannot stop—you will have a sense of tremendous power, power that is not yours but is coming from the whole group.

It's important to understand this as a basic mechanism for relating. Jesus speaks about this in the Bible as well: You cannot influence another person if you see that person as an object. If you can't get beyond objectification, then you are not treating other people as if they are human, and you are not acknowledging the field.

Fake magic is the conceit that *I can do all of this myself.* Anybody who says, "*I have the magic in me*" is either lying or evil. Real magic is knowing that you are accessing power as part of the greater whole, that you are connected to a group and forces higher than yourself. Nothing in the universe is permanent, or valuable, unless it's done in partnership.

CHAPTER 3

Part X

Understanding the Counterforce: Part X

Part X makes it impossible for you to get what you need from each domain. Part X claims to *be* the Life Force, or to give you access *to* it—but really Part X is the counterforce to the Life Force. It's the exact opposite of what you want, as it is the driving force trying to convince you to avoid life—meanwhile, if you *don't* avoid life, you become filled with spiritual power. Part X doesn't want this, so it will try to convince you that it is God. But it's not. Part X destroys the positive assets of the Life Force and weakens it.

Part X gives you problems you don't need to have and gives you solutions that make the problem worse. In fact, it will keep you in bigger and bigger problems. Part X convinces you that you need to have this problem. That's Evil.

Here are some simple examples of Part X at work. Let's say I'm nervous and a friend tells me that Xanax is very helpful for anxiety— so I develop a Xanax habit. Part X loves any medical intervention like this that's not about resolving the root problem. Let's say I have a competitive streak—Part X loves to feed me the idea that it's important for me to win, by any means, at any cost, whether it's financially or playing a game. I don't really need to play that game in the first place, and it doesn't avail me of anything, but Part X convinces me that winning will solve all of my problems. The classic example of "keeping up with the Joneses," buying a more expensive house or a second home to keep in step with friends and neighbors—that part of you that insists your life should get bigger, so the demands on your resources need to get bigger—is very much Part X. Eventually the whole thing collapses.

Part X controls us by saying, *I guarantee I can give you something that you can't get anywhere else. But what you have to give up to get this is the exact thing that's most important.* In the old days, we would say that you've sold your soul to the Devil. In modern times, we might say that you've sold your soul to capitalism.

Part X uses your desire to avoid all three unavoidables (Pain, Uncertainty, and the Need for Constant Work) as a weapon against you: It will sell you a bill of goods, so to speak, promising that under its direction, you can avoid pain, uncertainty, and hard work.

Part X is our ego on steroids. It will always work against us—its goal is to literally destroy your soul and co-opt your body. It constantly tries to co-opt our intuition as well for its own ends and desires.

Part X has two goals. One is destructive, and one is constructive. The destructive goal is to control the human soul. The Devil doesn't want to kill you. What good are you then? What he wants to do is neuter and enslave you, to use you for his purposes. If you are compulsively seeking things that don't exist, you'll not only never get them, you've already lost your soul. And that's what the Devil wants. He doesn't want your body. He'd be happy if you could live for two hundred years and spread his word.

The constructive goal of Part X involves free will. Part X can be a great teacher, and you can freely choose which meaning to give its lessons. You can even choose to make Part X your mentor, where it will put you under duress, injure you, and force you to heal.

This is the positive role of evil. In other words, when you meet evil, or Part X, your challenge is to view evil as a teacher and ask yourself, *What do I need? What are the instinctual habits and reflexes that I can develop to help me respond to the moments when Part X begins to take me over?* Even if you have doubts about this model, you must continue to trust that it will work—through faith and repetition, you will develop the reflexes to respond to Part X. As part of this training, you will have to give up certain things, a process which I call renunciation. Renunciation requires throwing out not just a singular victory, but the whole concept of victory. It's not that we want to lose; it's having the confidence to know that if we do lose, we have the tools we need to respond to the loss.

There's an old story in Faust where God and Lucifer are sitting next to each other, and Lucifer complains, "I always try to do bad, and it always ends up being good."

God allows Part X, or the Devil, to take over the human unconscious. He allows it because if you want to sharpen a knife, you need to sharpen it against something that's hard and rough. You don't sharpen a knife with a sponge. Nothing would happen. The friction is what forces your survival through instinct. You must accept this because it's not going away. This is where your opportunity comes to actually learn something and evolve.

As in a chess game, Part X wants to be one step ahead of you. This can make someone feel suicidal—they get so demoralized that they lose the instinctual sense that they can live productively. Suicide is a growth industry. It's crept into every nook and cranny in our culture because we've lost the ability to find meaning in everyday life. People feel that they have no future. No matter how fucked-up the average person is, on some level they want to learn, they want to advance, and they want to help other people. I call Part X the "avatar of impossibility," because it convinces people that these things are not possible.

Part X participates in loose talk on a deep level. Part X promises you that if you follow it and do what it tells you to do—lie, cheat, become a junkie, whatever it is—it will give you magical powers. Classically, the most magical power Part X promises is immortality itself. Don't buy it.

Even though Part X can be frenetic, hyperactive, and grandiose, think of it like a stop sign, preventing you from moving forward on your path. Part X will always try to trick you, even as it seems that it's teaching you to find the easy way out.

How to Deepen Your Relationship with Your Unconscious

The tools are designed to do something. They change how you process experiences, and what you think of both yourself and the future. But most importantly, they change the environment that you are in. Once you start to shift, even in the World of Small Things, the universe shifts around you. You start exercising, and somehow you attract someone you went to junior high school with, which is very stimulating. All of a sudden it becomes easier to write. Just taking one or two steps can create hope.

People sometimes say, "This is a very superficial and materialistic way of treating people's issues." But they're wrong. They're completely wrong, actually. It's the opposite: To make the unconscious partner with you, you have to get the unconscious to take action, to get that mechanism of movement going regardless of outcome. If you do this enough times, you gain confidence—not confidence that you're going to win in every circumstance in life, but that there's hope that it's possible. Part X is the avatar of impossibility, but if you can take someone through an experience that something is possible, even the smallest thing, you've changed their interpretation of the universe.

You want to deepen your relationship with your unconscious and functionally practice this process. One way to know that the unconscious is present is that it typically runs very deep, and when it gets stirred up and spit out, you experience it differently than you would your normal conscious material. It has a different quality. The unconscious is going to come out with less desire to compete, dominate, or have the illusion that it can control the world. The unconscious has a tremendous instinctual force, and yet it's completely unattached to the result, as impossible as that seems. If something happens that seems, in a million years, as if it couldn't happen—for example, that I am now a public figure, which I never would have predicted—it is at least partially coming from the unconscious.

It's important to try to get your unconscious material moving, and it's also important to try to connect with your Shadow, which is related to Part X. The Shadow is the embodiment of everything you feel insecure about, and Part X twists those unconscious insecurities and uses them to attack you.

The best approach to neutralizing Part X is basically to talk to your Shadow. Everything that has real agency in the whole universe has it because it's part of a pair, or part of a large group. There is absolutely nothing that you can do alone. So when you are talking to your Shadow, you are pairing up with it to resist the deceptions of Part X. You can absolutely use your Shadow as part of your field.

The unconscious tries to help you, but it does so by undermining your every belief. Jung tells a story about how a patient was being very stubborn, and this stubborn patient kept having the same dream over and over again. It was obvious that the patient was resisting something. In total, he had the same dream sixty times. So finally, the patient gave in and said, "Okay, I was wrong, and you were right—I'm resisting." The next day, he had a dream that was the exact opposite of the preceding dreams. I read this story when I was a kid, and it blew my mind, but now it makes perfect sense to me. The unconscious can only give you information when it simultaneously destroys your conscious instincts. It does this because the human ego is very strong. If it doesn't undermine your ego, you will think you know what you're talking about.

It's not about interpreting the dream correctly, or even giving it a specific meaning; it's not about making sense of it or proving it. If something spiritual wants to send you a message, it can't send you that message until you've lost the basic sense that you're right. The dream world doesn't particularly care if the facts that it appears to be revealing are true or not true. Dealing with the unconscious is a collective, interactive, and somewhat chaotic undertaking. When I was young, a psychoanalyst would say, "It means this," and another psychoanalyst would say, "No, it means this." I knew I was dealing with bit players who didn't know a thing. The correct attitude is "I don't know shit." The unconscious is not a goal-directed process.

I'm going to explain H.I.P.A. to you in a bit (see p. 110), where the "I" stands for "ignorance." You want to stay ignorant, not because you want to be wrong, but because you want to know that you don't know. This is one of the primary ways to identify that something is coming from the unconscious. Because if it's coming from the conscious mind, and it's *Go to the Bahamas,* or *Buy this dress,* or *Fall in love with this woman,* then that's regular consciousness talking. But if it comes out like a surprising gift, where you can have dinner with it, but if you put it in your mouth it will explode, that's the unconscious. You won't be able to find your footing. Because when you find your footing, it means you've found the place where you think you know what's going on, and God doesn't like that. God shouldn't like it, because there's much more to the universe and to your own psyche than you even want to admit.

The other good way to identify the unconscious is that sometimes you'll get a very intense, almost undeniable instinct. It's like a judgment call, but it doesn't come from your thinking. It's God.

Exercise: Identifying the Unconscious with Three Moves

1. **WRITE**: In the myth of Medusa and Perseus, Perseus is unable to look Medusa in the face, because she turns all men to stone. So Perseus polishes the inside of his shield until it's like a mirror, and he slays her by coming in backwards. Writing is like a giant mirror; it reflects back at you what's happening in your unconscious. Most people will say, "Bullshit—why is something chaotic in a dream? Why is that more valuable than my everyday consciousness or my everyday associations?" And the answer is that things you don't have strict control over tend to bring better

information—not worse, but better. And the reason is that Part X can't fuck with it, because it can't get its hands on it. So writing about what you think is going wrong with you is good, even if you're wrong.

2. **DO SOMETHING CREATIVE**: It doesn't matter what type of activity you choose; anything creative will wake the unconscious up really nicely. It doesn't matter if what comes out is shit—keep going. It's like activating a certain muscle.

3. **TEST YOUR TENTACLES**: When you meet a person, specifically someone you don't know well, test out your tentacles, which is the most intuitive psychic part of yourself. Do this without any specific goal in mind. Go inside the other person's aura and then come out. Most of what you experience in life is not A or B; it's an interaction, the field between two people who are acting on each other. So what you're trying to do is develop and risk trusting your own intuition with other people. You're using these tools to get a more accurate and complete feeling about the human environment. The signature of the universe has more to do with the unconscious than it does with the conscious. Think of it as a space, or a place that you want to enter as many times as you can, much like the Plane of Will (see p. 114). This isn't about proving your psychic abilities or that you're "right"; it's simply about exercising your intuition and making it a practice to feel into your environment all the time. We'll talk more about swallowing your doubt in the section on Uncertainty, when we talk about the Instinct Cycle (see p. 95).

P.R.I.M.

The acronym P.R.I.M. represents the four aspects of Part X—Past, Reward, Injury, and Must. Knowing these will help you recognize

Part X at work. Identifying these signs doesn't require any kind of advanced knowledge that Part X is coming; you simply have to be familiar with certain prototypical behaviors in order to see what's happening.

PAST: Close your eyes and find a time or a place in your life when you couldn't get out of the loop. Next, visualize: *What is the effect of this symptom on my life now?* The P in P.R.I.M. stands for "past," which is the tendency to repeat behaviors and, worse, thoughts, over and over and over again. We do this because they're familiar. You might think that you're finding yourself, that you're recovering a long-lost part of yourself, but it's a Trojan Horse. The past is not coming back, but you can keep talking about it forever. Is there an unconscious drive to live in that world, even though it doesn't exist anymore? Bring yourself back to the present. People like to look at patterns as a source of meaning. Patterns are helpful in the smaller world: Going to the gym, eating a healthy breakfast—so long as they are done without the illusion of some symbolic prize or reward, these can be useful habits, but not when you are using them to explain your life. Doing this says more about Part X's role in your life, as Part X hates you to have any freedom at all. Part X creates a style of thinking that feels like unbreakable patterns. People like familiarity, so they like anything inside themselves that they can repeat. If they can repeat it easily, they mistake it for real action. Real action is the opposite—real action must be taken into a void. You do not need to resolve anything in your past; Part X is simply keeping you in a loop.

REWARD: A false magical reward says, *You can have an easy life; you can get whatever you want or need. All you have to do is buy my product.* This is a lie. Many very successful and wealthy people, who can buy whatever they want, are very unhappy. That said, don't mistake these false rewards for ordinary material things; Part X is selling you a belief, the idea that this reward can make you superhuman. But here's the secret: There is no secret. You'll never be able to transcend the laws of the physical world; however, when you commit to the behaviors and the tools outlined in this book, you will develop superpowers. Why? How is it different? The difference is that you've added a collective element—you are working with higher forces. Your potential must be realized as part of a group (see p. 25).

INJURY: Besides getting punched in the face, there is no injury that is not narcissistic—by this I mean that most injuries are an affront to your ego, which will then tell you that you've been wronged. Think of a narcissistic injury as an accusation or suggestion of some bad quality you have, or a claim about something you did wrong, which someone makes against you and that hurts you. Everyone has a Geiger counter inside them that measures what's happened to them: *This person owes me an apology; that person owes me twenty dollars,* and so forth. This becomes an endless cycle in your mind of everything that's owed to you. I call it the Maze (see p. 67). People believe they can scream, yell, and prove that someone owes them something because they don't think life is fair. The injured party collects injuries: They may complain about them, but they do not really want to correct them. Some people harbor a desire to be injured. This is because when you're injured, you have something to complain about, and to that degree, you identify yourself with the injury. This is a form of victimhood. Part X wants attention any way it can get it—if it can't get positive attention, it will settle for negative.

MUST: "Must" is the compelling drive to do something impulsively. Part X uses this to dominate you. It is a superhuman evil—it might drive you to do drugs, get in a big fight with your spouse, or waste money. It doesn't matter what the compelling drive is, but it must be decided and acted upon very quickly. The driver behind this sort of action is a fake Life Force. We will talk about "must" more in the following pages, but one of my quick defenses against it is: *I don't need that.* Not that I wouldn't like it, or wouldn't take it, but I don't need it. This speaks directly against "must."

Phil's Story: Childhood Gambling

Unlike most of the city's playgrounds, the one I grew up in had a very specific quality: It was infected by gambling. But it also had some great basketball players, most of whom were Jewish like me.

The older guys would bet on the younger ones who just wanted to play ball. Betting was a very common habit, which eventually led to more expensive, more corrupt gambling later in life.

This was a common scenario among the kids I grew up with: Someone would say, "Hey, do this little job for me—I'm not sure it'll even work, but if it does, I'll give you five thousand dollars." Then another guy would come up and say, "I'll give you fifty dollars, but it's going to be very exciting." Even though the first job paid $4,950 more, kids would pick the guy who was paying $50. The first time I saw this happen, I couldn't believe it. But it shows the power of "must": A gambler has to have the excitement.

In my practice, I've seen three different patients who have lost a hundred million dollars gambling. The impulse to gamble is driven by forces that don't really have anything to do with gambling, or with the future. There is no future. In their compulsive search for excitement, gamblers are not free or full of life; quite the opposite. They are driven by a fake Life Force. They can't stop because they're afraid they will die otherwise.

"Must" energy is a subtle force that can trap anyone—not just gamblers or "bad people"—in compulsive behaviors. It might manifest as workaholism, addiction to substances or food, or overuse of social media. We all have a Part X within us, and this part uses "must" to strip away our free will, driving us to act on impulse without realizing it. When fully under its control, we act not out of choice but because we feel we can't stop ourselves. Recognizing Part X's influence is crucial to regaining control. The Life Force helps counter this energy by reminding us that we don't need to follow those compulsions. This awareness doesn't come from the intellect but from instinct. You'll know it's a "must" energy when no matter what actually happens, the only part of it that you care about, or that feels connected to your identity, is the "must" energy.

When you are fully trapped by "must," you are doing things out of impulse, not for any reason other than that you cannot not do them. Most people don't realize they're at that point until it's too late. P.R.I.M. gives us a set of parameters to describe Part X and how it operates, as nothing is as important as developing an ability to recognize Part X's presence and its dangers. When I'm struggling with "must," I say to myself, *I don't need that.* This is the assertion of the Life Force. You won't know on an intellectual level if you're driven by "must." You can only know it on an instinctual level.

HITLER AND EVIL

There is a macro evil which you may not meet within the scope of your own life. It is different but related to Part X. This macro evil goes beyond simply attacking the freedom or independence in your personal life and helping to strengthen your character when you overcome it. This kind of evil has no constructive purpose besides asserting its power and control over other human beings or whole countries. Macro evil is controlled by some other force, a force that is inhuman and does not have human needs or wants. You can think of this as capital-E Evil, with many junior devils serving it. One of these junior devils was Adolf Hitler.

In 1933, a young reporter in her twenties from New York was in Berlin when Hitler was coming into power. She reported that before this guy Hitler spoke, he was almost hiding in a corner of the room. He looked so weak as a person, she was surprised he could even stand up. But after he was introduced, his body posture changed. He became more vertical. Everybody in the hall went crazy. It was as if he was animated by some other force. This was one reporter's experiential reflection, not based on any system of belief or any foreknowledge of what Hitler would go on to do. She said he spoke for about half an hour, and the crowd was banging on the tables and screaming by the end. When his speech was over, he went back to where he had started and turned into a little mouse again.

That is real evil. He wasn't even himself. He was a meal for the Devil.

CHAPTER 4

Universe One and Universe Two

Concepts for Understanding the Structure of Reality

There are two points of view, or conceptual frameworks, for understanding the universe or what reality really is. The value in Universe One is defined by mathematics. Anything dominated by mathematics, whether it's a culture or a religion, eventually becomes completely money driven. The bottom-line value is money. In Universe One, nobody is satisfied, and the field is very narrow. People are pissed, because someone else is getting more than they're getting. Money, in itself, cannot create what you need, and you end up with all kinds of conflict. Higher forces do not exist in Universe One because they cannot be quantified—in Universe One, you cannot access them. No matter what happens in Universe One, even if you make all the money in the world, you end up feeling like a loser, because the only real value is in Universe Two, where you must create something.

Universe Two is a very different playing field. In Universe Two, money means nothing. Outcomes mean nothing. The only thing that matters in Universe Two is the present: this moment. The value of Universe Two is creativity. The most valuable thing you can do is to create something out of nothing.

I once knew a woman who was an exceptional kindergarten teacher. She worked in a public school on the Upper West Side of Manhattan and word about her spread: More and more parents came to her for guidance, even parents of kids who were in other grades, to ask her for hints on how to teach their children so they could get into fancier and better schools. Naturally, somebody said, "You should start your own business, because you're getting paid two dollars a year to do this."

Eventually, she quit and started her own business to make more money. What she had been doing was really purposeful: What could be more purposeful than teaching a little kid how to read? But in Universe One, the Devil convinces you that money is the most important thing. The world doesn't need her to have a $9 million apartment on Central Park West. It's nice and all, but the world doesn't need that. The world needs her to teach five-year-olds. But people don't think that way, because the symbology of money in Universe One is that it's magic. Working your ass off, making $61,000 a year, and retiring isn't as good as the fantasy of Universe One.

If you want to know who you really are, ask yourself what you would spend your time on even if you knew it would never make you any money.

If you're willing to give up part of your income for something else, whatever it is, then you've discovered your higher power. For example, I lose money when I work on developing these books, because I can't see as many patients. When you find something to spend your time on even when no money is present, that's a sign that you're leaving Universe One and entering Universe Two. Your Life Force is revealing itself to you. How much "power" you acquire depends on which universe you think you're living in—and by "power" I mean the word in its broadest sense, which is the power to create, the strongest power on earth. Your real values—and what you choose to do to serve those values—make up the job the universe needs you to do, but money really fucks the whole thing up. People's relationship to money is a direct relationship to social status. "Social status" is not even a strong enough term to describe this phenomenon, because people actually think money makes them inherently superior to other people.

In general, most of us lack the real spiritual power required to see the Devil clearly, and to at least get away from him. Because of mass media, and the propaganda coming at us like a shitstorm, there are so few people left with any sense of what is right and what is wrong. And I don't mean that in a moral sense.

We feel that the twenty guys who are worth billions are corrupting the world. But they're not the only corrupting force. What's corrupting is the guy who lives across the street from you who became an investment banker and makes $2.5 million a year. Let's say you're a great surgeon, but you only make one million dollars. It might sound venal to define it this way, but this doctor likely feels he's being undervalued, and he's tempted to do something else with his time to multiply that million into a billion. This is Universe One.

There are now doctors who don't really see patients anymore—their work is done via an abstract game where machines become the arbiters of diagnosis and treatment. There is good that comes from this technology, but it also crushes people's souls. Everybody expects lawyers to be corrupt, but it's disappointing to see it also happen in medicine. In the early seventies, it became kosher for lawyers to advertise—I remember seeing my first billboard for an ambulance-chasing lawyer back then and thinking, *Holy shit, the world is over.* It wasn't, as there was so much more corruption to come, but it was the beginning of something different. That type of advertising now extends to the healing arts. Encountering it for the first time was kind of like seeing your parents having sex. I kept thinking, *Am I actually seeing this? This seems wrong.* We're now at a point in our culture where tremendous financial success in itself is not sufficient for people. There's a saying in Hollywood that holds across our culture: It's not enough to win; your friends have to lose as well. This is the sickness of Universe One. Universe One is cold. It has no specific emotional or spiritual life, or connection with the human race. In Part X's view of the world, we're no more important than stones—the chemists and biologists, many of whom typify the values of Universe One, will tell you that there's nothing beyond us except a bunch of rocks. There are no higher forces, just an impersonal and empty universe. A strict rationalism denies the reality of Universe Two.

Universe Two is the complete opposite of Universe One. Because it's not mathematically based, it can't be described or measured. In Universe Two, value is based on creation—and not what you created in junior high, or last year, or even ten years ago. It's based on the act of creation as an ongoing process. You're only really creating value for yourself if you're doing something right now, at this moment. That is the only power that can reach a human being.

If you're stuck in Universe One, you've given up. You've sold your soul to the Devil: You've given up on the most complex, most brilliant, and most indispensable part of the universe, which is the evolution of human beings. God doesn't give a shit if you went to Harvard, or worked at Goldman Sachs, or won a Nobel Prize. God doesn't care if you have job A, B, or C—God only cares that you not quit.

Universe Two is a level of consciousness, along with a level of suppositions and value sensing—all of it invisible, and none of it able to be proven. But it's a broader, more spiritual space in your mind.

Human beings are God's hobby, you could say. He doesn't care about anything else. The only thing God cares about is encouraging humans to reach up and look for the higher level of Universe Two—the spiritual part of you needs to breathe in some of this level. You can't do it with thoughts and concepts, and you certainly can't do it with mathematics or anything hierarchical. Why? Because you're playing against yourself, not playing against anybody else. If you're not working toward what is innate to you, then it doesn't matter—you can kill someone else financially, but it has no meaning. Meaning has to be discovered inside of you, and this meaning is very specific.

Some people can sense that they're on some sort of mission. God didn't give them a printout that says, *Here's why you're being incarnated into this world.* He wants something different. He wants people to get to know themselves through their own individual efforts.

The interesting thing about human development is that there are two paths to success. There's a merit system, and there's a power system—again, by power I mean real creative power, not symbolic or fake power. The merit system requires moving along the beaten path that everyone else has already worked. In one graduating class at Princeton, something like two-thirds of the seniors wanted to go into investment banking. There's nothing dishonest about being an investment banker, but that career path typically has two motivations: making money and beating other people. The experience you'll have in the merit system will leave you bored and unfulfilled. If you're living within this Universe One world, you can't be satisfied, because it's dry and has no space in which to provide you with a sense of meaning. It lacks imagination, courage, and real immersion in the world around you. Some people are passionate about careers and self-expression that take them on the merit path, which is fine. But anyone who has other Universe One motivations is taking something from the soul.

The power system, on the other hand, offers no preordained path. There's no one person to look at, study, or follow. You can see this in kids, who move in this system naturally: They're not in the business of trying to control forces or engineering their lives. They are simply living in the power system, which has no markers to tell you whether you're winning or not. It's quintessentially made out of uncertainty. People ask, *Well, if it's uncertain, how can I succeed?* Success on this path can be achieved, but it does not define the system. The power system runs on instinct. It is the only truly creative way.

Universe One and the Biphasic Fantasy

The biphasic fantasy is the mentality of Universe One.

The biphasic fantasy is not for somebody who merely wants to succeed in life, because that's not enough. The biphasic fantasy is for someone who wants to be God. And the only way they can be God is by defeating every other living, breathing soul around them. There's a problem, though. You've defeated everybody; the battlefield is empty; everyone is dead. And you're thinking, *I'm great. I conquered all.* But then, a little birdie says, *You didn't do that yourself, you lying fuck. You went for the fake magic, or a lie about what the universe really is.*

Goodness, or acceptance, or being in love, are basically negatives in the biphasic fantasy. This is because they're pleasing temporarily, but they're not a "real" accomplishment; they're symbolic. Of course, they have tremendous meaning, but the idea of what is meaningful is crippled because it's competitive and comparative and bound to Universe One.

After you've won, and you're God, there's immediately an erosion because those good feelings start to feel fake. You think, *Wait, this success is too big for me to kid myself and say I did it all by myself.* Eventually, you completely lose the feeling that you've conquered or won anything—and so you use the biphasic fantasy to rev yourself up again and give yourself the illusion that maybe you are God.

It's called the biphasic fantasy because you start out with the alienation phase where you think it's you against the world. Alienation means *I now have a chance to become God. I only have that chance because the odds are stacked against me.* It's like John Wayne riding into the O.K. Corral where there are twenty-two guys on the other team. Nobody would go see that movie if the odds were even. That's part of the drama. *Everyone's against me, but I won anyway.*

The problem with the biphasic fantasy is that you have to keep reproducing the alienation, because if you stop being such a victim, it's impossible for it to be you against the world. It doesn't work if the world starts to come onto your team. Most people are not aware of this. But if someone gets into the position where they are not able to accept success, it's the biphasic fantasy at play: They don't want to accept success because they can't play the game anymore. Whatever they've done or accomplished, they need to destroy, so they can play the game again. That's why you see people in show business do crazy things and blow up their careers. When I ask them why they do this, they usually say, "It was boring." I try to push them to become accepting of a world that has less drama in it.

This also happens primarily with men, who don't understand

how to relate and are alienated. Some women look down on men as if they're idiots; unfortunately, they're often correct. Jung's wife wrote a book that no man could ever write, but because she was a woman, she could say whatever she wanted to about women. She said that women were screwing themselves up because they were trying to gain power by acting the way they think a man would act, and that they were not good at it. And why should they be? Jung's wife said that women had to renounce the kind of pleasure that they thought men were getting from domination, because men were not actually getting pleasure; they were committing suicide.

For the most part, women look down on men as if they're stupid because men are competing all day long in the biphasic fantasy to win, whereas women have already won, even if that's not yet clear in our modern-day power structures. Women are infinitely more powerful, and there's nothing men can do about it—they can create life. Women aren't necessarily thinking about that all the time, but they've likely felt it. Women have access to the ultimate creative experience. Not every woman actually has a child, but women feel the ability to create. So they look at all the machinations that the male psyche or the male soul goes through, and it seems like the fake version. Generally speaking, women intuitively understand Universe Two.

As a human being of either sex, you have a choice. You can either stay in touch with God, or you can try to be God. It took me years to understand that.

Universe One is a way of thinking that gives you the feeling that you are either winning or losing. Universe One is a way of looking at the world where people tell themselves they can be God.

Universe Two is a way of looking at the world where you no longer have to compete to discover who you really are. Universe Two trains you in a way of looking at the world where value lies in your ability to create.

PART II

CHAPTER 5

The Three Unavoidables

I t's time to enter the three domains and contend with the three un-avoidables in life: Pain, Uncertainty, and the Need for Constant Work. Each of these domains makes a demand that you must meet, and each domain is a component of the Y, which brings them to-gether in unity. Finding balance in the Y is a creative unlock. A suc-cessful life is the ability to create, and only by living that life will you feel you are reaching out to become who you really are.

The universe is fully conscious—and the universe wants to make a personal connection with you. But in order to do that, you have to go into these three arenas that hurt to deal with—your laziness and fear, whipped up by Part X, will try to convince you that you can and should avoid these domains. It sounds old-fashioned, but you must accept these domains and God into your life. God does not enter your life in a way that's comfortable. He enters it in the form of these challenges. The three domains in aggregate make up the face of God. In each domain, the face of God is going to challenge you. The de-mand is: *Are you going to keep avoiding?*

As Rudolf Steiner says, whoever or whatever created the universe created something out of nothing. Steiner says that when you're crossing the threshold from this level of consciousness to a higher consciousness, you will experience tremendous resistance. A whole cadre of spiritual beings will keep you from crossing the threshold. This is necessary because if you crossed the threshold without learning to contend with this resistance, you would be taken over by evil.

You will never conquer your laziness and fear—and that's not the goal. You must learn to live with them, and move forward despite them, to resist the temptation of avoidance, which is what laziness and fear promise. When you are able to get the three domains working simultaneously, you unlock the Y. It's not just that you need to put the three together to achieve the total potential of a human being; it's that the universe wants human beings to have these superpowers. Meeting the demands of the three domains systematically— and resisting avoidance—is the only way to keep yourself from falling back into the void. The only way to get these superpowers is to face your laziness or fear. Each domain presents itself as an obstacle so that you can do this, because the universe insists that you evolve. In order to do that, you must face these three domains and bring them to a point, to a unifying trinity, over and over again.

Engaging with the domains will change your experience of life and unblock your ability to create. I'm not suggesting you need to be someone who is "creative" in the traditional sense. The promise of this training program is that it helps you resist and remove the obstacles that hold back your abilities, whatever they might be.

God set all of this up to force you to become your most potent self. One tool can't do it. Even ten tools can't do it. This training program is more than a set of tools; it is a philosophy. Philosophically, everyone needs training in the way the universe works. Again, the details are a little bit different in each of the domains, but the universe, or God, or whatever you want to call it, is basically saying, *You can become my peer, and you can all get power in this way. You can have the power of God.* But the development of that kind of power comes only when you stop avoiding. The whole human race— certainly in the West—is convinced that it can have magic and simultaneously be comfortable. But it doesn't work like that.

Here is a spiritual law that bears repeating: **The exact things that you will do anything to avoid are the same things you need to make progress.**

Because we're all connected, one or two people using the tools can influence the entire group—and they won't even know they're being influenced. In fact, you don't even have to know, or care, if you're influencing them.

This is not a training program where you have a problem, you use a tool, and the problem goes away, at least temporarily. That's fine, but that's kindergarten. To really unlock the power described in this book, to achieve healing and personal spiritual power, you need a protocol, because all of the pieces are linked. You don't necessarily have to believe in the underlying philosophy, but follow the practical steps as if there's some validity in what I'm saying, and watch what happens.

What's Blocking You from Realizing Your Potential?

This process is designed so that you can experience your potential every second of your life. Still, the price you pay for this ongoing and undefinable achievement is to contend with the three unavoidable domains: Pain, Uncertainty, and the Need for Constant Work. And keep in mind that you're never done; there's no end point. But the fact that there's no end point is good.

The universe is infinite, and in turn, you're making an infinite commitment to do something. The fact that this is so difficult, and that you must keep doing it, is part of the experience of immortality.

Human beings have a limitless potential—a super potential. The word "potential" is overused and does not have much meaning, primarily because people think of it as a fixed point. In reality, it is unrealized—it is a process that unfolds, not an object of achievement. Potential becomes fake magic when it is a static entity. Realizing potential is available to everyone, but it comes with a price. The main way you get access to this super potential is in the face of certain disasters, glitches, or failures. It's a bit like being initiated into a greater level of ability. If you can do something that you thought was impossible, that you didn't think you could do, it is much more life-changing than a thousand psychoanalytic sessions. Why? Because it requires some kind of internal revelation or change. It would be very unusual to change just one thing in your life and not create a lot of other changes. Doing the previously impossible is part of a process, which is important to understand, because your super potential must constantly change and evolve. It is not forever earned, and it doesn't last. It's not as though you get your SAG card and then you're done as an actor, across the finish line. You have to maintain your potential and grow, or it will fall apart.

Potential is very real—and it's out there—but the work it takes to realize it is not much fun. It's even less fun to hold onto it. It's not about winning, but that's because you'll never "win" or "finish" and if anybody tells you that you will, they're full of shit. Because it's the opposite in reality. If you want to reach your potential, you will suffer.

Human beings are capable of the most incredible things, but they first have to accept reality: The playing field is unpleasant. The organization of the universe—and certainly the organization of a human life—has meaning and purpose and direction. But it won't reveal itself to you if you choose to avoid the things you don't like.

The universe is constructed with each person having a mission, which is not a dramatic thing. It's like putting a jigsaw puzzle together—all of the little pieces, with their unique missions, find their place. You're supposed to advance your potential, while simultaneously accepting the fact that if this is the whole world, every single person has a niche. If you don't find your niche, you won't be whole. And if you're not whole in this area, you won't achieve total wholeness.

When you use the tools enough, a cosmic pathway is revealed. It's not revealed to you as a bunch of facts or theories or cognitive material. What's revealed to you is something that you really need to know and feel—it's your personal pathway, a pathway of life right through the universe. But that's not enough, as Part X will be there with you the whole time, giving you problems and screwing everything up. Staying on the pathway—in the tents—is difficult (see p. 19).

The ability to harvest potential comes with a big headache and no fun. People want to avoid it, but what they're avoiding is the key to the whole thing—if they follow the bouncing blue ball, it will make them extraordinary. That's the way the universe is constructed.

Let me ask you: What have you sacrificed to avoid these things that you cannot avoid? When you live in avoidance, in the Realm of Illusion, Part X convinces you that you can live in fairy-tale land. This comes at a very high cost. God is interested in the evolution of the human race. God doesn't care if you get an A or a B or a C. But if you quit, then God will be upset. Embracing this truth allows you to have meaning that's both relevant to you and to what your instincts are telling you, and relative to God's efforts to shape the human being. It is both individual and collective. The universe God has built forces you to stop avoiding.

Real power means you've made a real impact on the world, whether it's on your children or in the wider culture. If you feel that you don't have the power to create something that has real impact, you're going to be perpetually unhappy. We all need to fully develop our own individual potential in order to battle Part X and battle collective evil. We're all needed in the war.

Fake power has to do with credentials, wearing the right brand of shoe, hanging out with the right people, choosing a career based on how much money you will make. There's nothing bad about those things, but they're dangerous if you don't have something higher or deeper involved, where you can have the sense that *this is me*. You have to go by your instincts, because the only way to come to answers to questions like *Who am I? What's my mission? What am I doing here? What are the obstacles going to be?* is by taking action. There's no other way. The rest is speculative. No philosophy has any efficacy or juice to it on its own—it can't have an impact unless it ends in action.

Exercise: A Goal You Doubt You Can Achieve

Growth is always available to some degree. But for whatever reason, we come to most of the important things in our lives with a great deal of anxiety and not a whole lot of confidence. The concept of developing yourself reflects the fact that the human organism is built to expand and to learn. If you can't feel or imagine any reality related to this, you'll never touch your potential.

Pick a goal in your life which you have grave doubts about your ability to reach. Suggest to yourself that you have the potential to succeed in this area, solve this problem, or develop this skill, even if you don't believe it. Close your eyes and see yourself actually taking the step. See what it looks like. Your brain can't tell the difference, so if you can feel any bit of that potential, you will start to activate it.

THE REALM OF ILLUSION

Here's a typical story in my practice. A young actor comes to see me, maybe about twenty-two years old, who has moved to Los Angeles. He is talented, but he has horrible habits. He doesn't get enough sleep, he uses drugs, and he has six girlfriends. Honestly, it could be any number of things—I've seen it all.

I would tell him, "You're talented and you're good looking, but if you continue with these bad habits, you're going to fail."

He would respond, "No, I'll clean up my act, but only after I become a big star. I don't want to work that hard until the rewards are coming in."

My response: "You're a spoiled fucking asshole." So once in a million years, the kid with the bad habits succeeds, at least temporarily. So now he's a big star. People recognize him on the street, but he notices that nothing is different, except he maybe gets a better table at a restaurant. But nothing real has changed at all.

He shows up back in my office and says, "I've done my part; I've become a big star. But life isn't easy. I thought my reward was entering the magic world." But really he is in the Realm of Illusion.

He believed in a fairy tale that if he hit mark A, B, C, or D

REALM OF ILLUSION

SNAPSHOT

REAL LIFE

TURD

in show business, he'd be lifted out of the world of normal people where you have to obey these rules.

When someone resists the truth—"I don't have to obey these rules anymore"—that's very dangerous, particularly for their mental health. This type of person tends to have high suicidal ideation. They have a sense of being put-upon: "How could you not give me this magical reward?"

The answer to that question is: "I can't, because it doesn't exist. Nobody fucking gets that. Nobody."

IN OUR REALITY, there are two kinds of magic: fake magic, which is the Realm of Illusion and attached to Universe One, and real magic, which cannot work through any individual. You cannot possess real magic only for yourself, and you cannot possess it at all without entering the domains. This is the magic of Universe Two, which is connected to creativity as it emerges in the moment, not as a fixed state or idea.

Something is fake when the ego says, *I can do this without help*. True magic is the opposite; it says, *I can't do anything without the partnership of the universe*. From here, you must remain humble, because it's not totally up to you.

Thanks to the nature of my career in Hollywood, I've seen many people who believe they can live in the Realm of Illusion. But this doesn't just affect movie stars and creative executives. It affects all of us who are convinced by Universe One that if we go to the right college, get the right job, marry the right person, have a lot of followers on social media, and make a certain amount of money, we're done. These people are convinced they can have a soft, magical life—that they're owed that. I call the Realm of Illusion, the unreal world that most of us live in, the "snapshot world," because it has no movement in it, and there's no depth. The search for magical perfection doesn't exist. The snapshot world doesn't exist. The rules are harsh, and you will get hurt, but they will also reward you with real magic.

The story above about the young actor is not atypical for me. When I was seeing a full slate of patients, I would get many guys like this—and sometimes they would become my best patients. One actor, who was about thirty at the time and already famous, came in. He sat down, and I made it a point not to seem impressed, which I wasn't. We talked for a bit, then he got up and walked out. His feelings were hurt. Four years later, he came back and became one of my best patients. The first time, he wasn't ready, as he refused to come out of the Realm of Illusion. These guys become ready when they have a big success. They're convinced that it will give them a different set of experiences, but it doesn't. They thought they would feel different, or better, but they don't. Something is missing. Part X loves putting people in the Realm of Illusion, in a world that doesn't exist—it's Part X's biggest weapon. Part X convinces you that within the magical Realm of Illusion, you'll succeed and get a prize—but it's a booby prize. There's nothing. You win a contest designed to win you nothing—and that's if you "succeed." Most people don't succeed at all.

The Realm of Illusion is a common place for people to go with their careers, and it's also common for patients to think that a partner will save them—they see their partners as having magical abilities, but really, it's false magic. I think of it as false magic because they're convinced that the relationship will save them from needing constant work. They become convinced the partner holds a key that can help them both avoid and escape the three domains, and that all of their issues will be solved.

My advice to patients who are doing this is to remind them that it's false magic, and that there is a misperception on their part. They can have the relationship; they just need to be honest with themselves that they need to contribute on a realistic basis to what the other person needs. There is no exoneration from pain, uncertainty, or the need for constant work.

False magic is anything that convinces you that the Realm of Illusion is real—to that end, false magic is anything that puts you in the Realm of Illusion in the first place. You can only access real magic by accepting the demands of the three domains. Real magic is a source of energy that you can touch but you'll never own; it's a source of energy that you can shape but never control. You must work, run really, to stay in constant touch with it. God has rewarded the human race with the ability to borrow the immense power of the universe—but you cannot make that connection if you avoid. You must submit to the demands of the three domains.

Exercise: Where Have You Tried to Exonerate Yourself?

What have you committed to, or tried to commit to, with the promise that if achieved, it will solve all of your problems? When have you convinced yourself that you can or should be exonerated from one of these three domains? What is the important thing that you are avoiding?

The Safety Zone

Patient Story: Fighter Pilot

I once had an unusual patient who was a psychiatrist himself. He had heard about the tools and wanted to get back in touch with a euphoria he had felt much earlier in his life. He had grown up with a borderline mother who was very ill—she was Part X personified, intent on co-opting him to her will. Sometimes she wouldn't let him go to school because she wanted company. She broke his will repeatedly. She'd curse him out and say anything to weaken him so he couldn't leave her. He would have fantasies where he'd have a machine gun and there would be a hundred enemies in front of him—he would machine gun them all down until they were dead and he could go to sleep. In 1951, during the Korean War, he was drafted into the Air Force. He was very smart, he tested great, and he got into a training program for fighter pilots. It was very dangerous work; people died on the aircraft carrier all the time. But he felt completely euphoric for those three years. He was a fantastic pilot, he could evade detection, and he had guns to protect himself. He felt good when he was connected to his fantasies but great when he was connected to something real. He could approach any girl without fear and talk to her. This was a complete 180 from his previous life, when he could barely leave his bedroom.

Then the war ended and he was discharged, which was a tragedy for him. For a year or two he went right back to the pattern with his mother. When she died, he was finally given his freedom, and went on to medical school and had a really nice life. He came to me before he died because he wanted me to help him restore himself to that level of courage and euphoria, to understand what it meant.

The war had been an intervention to take him right out of the Safety Zone his mother had confined him to—and he thrived. He was given explicit permission, or orders, to violate the expectations and laws and rules he had grown up under. But without that express permission, it took him the rest of his life to practice getting out of the Safety Zone.

What Is the Safety Zone?

We all recognize the Safety Zone. We're held there by fear, which is a version of pain. You want to get out but it's in your way, pushing you back in. If you keep having capitulations to your fear, eventually things start to feel impossible. You withdraw fully into the Safety Zone. The goal is to break through this wall, to get to the other side.

The Safety Zone is an obstacle—each of the three domains has an obstacle in it, and each domain also contains a power that you earn if you overcome the obstacle.

Avoidance means that you want to stay back from the world; you'd rather stay in the Safety Zone because the world seems too frightening. But as each domain will teach you, it's going to be worse if you keep avoiding life.

When people are afraid, I tell them that they can be as afraid as they want. Don't even think about not being afraid. Just go and do the thing and see what happens. Imagine a tightrope: If you slip, it's a forty-foot fall onto cement. Two people are going to walk the rope.

The first person is fixated on the idea that they might fall and really worried about it. The second person says, *I'm just going to take one step, and then another step, and then another step. I have no opinion about this tightrope at all.* Ask yourself a question: Who do you think is going to do better?

If you need to do something, especially if it requires action, the more time you allow to elapse before you take action (which includes using a tool), the more your self-esteem goes down. If you wait a really long time, you end up being altogether paralyzed.

If you leave the Safety Zone, you're going to face pain. In fact, this is the definition of the Safety Zone. Pain is the name we give to those moments when we're outside of it. But to make any sort of progress in life, we must face pain. We all know this on some level—birth itself is painful. But then life unfolds, and we're taught to avoid pain, that it's possible to learn how to avoid pain. Part X definitely tells us that it's possible, but it's not. When that fear of pain crystallizes into avoidance, we find ourselves in the Safety Zone.

Someone's fear, or insistence on avoiding pain, changes their whole life. How many opportunities did you turn down or resist because you were scared?

I call this the "law of pain" or "law of fear," which means that if you go right into the pain or fear, it diminishes. If you back off and are scared of it, it becomes too late to take action—when you are avoidant, the fear becomes large and toxic. To give you an easy example, let's say you have a single, next-door neighbor whom you're attracted to. If three years go by and you don't work up the nerve to borrow a cup of sugar from this person, you're going to be so frightened, you'll never do it. You'll be paralyzed.

So how are you going to get out of the Safety Zone?

Speed is the first law to get you out of the Safety Zone. The more time you allow to elapse without taking action, the weaker, less confident, and more frightened you become. Your heart literally gets weaker. When your life situation requires action, you want to take immediate action, even if it just involves using a tool. For example, as soon as you realize that a single and attractive woman has moved in next door, you introduce yourself or make an offer of something.

The action could be as simple as being extra nice to people. Whatever it is, just take action, quickly. The average person, especially the one who is depressed, waits too long before acting. In this philosophy, you don't have to wait for anything. Once you ascertain that there's something you must do, don't let time elapse, or you might become weaker and your confidence will go down. Take immediate action, not impulsive action.

To keep yourself from avoiding, you need to contact the most primitive part of yourself, which is the instinct. Things are moving too fast and they're too profound for the intellect to make any difference. Your unconscious is present, though. Think about it as a system: It's impossible to establish the real change you want unless you're willing to give up the pseudo-safety that you *think* you have but don't. Because everything in the universe travels and impacts everything else faster than we can think, taking immediate action requires getting in touch with the animal part of you. The reason is because the battle of fear is fought on this level, not on the level of intellect.

If you knock on your neighbor's door, it doesn't just give you a chance to have a date with somebody. It changes the whole way you look at the world. You build trust in yourself. When you pretend as if you are going to do something, or when you talk about doing something, and you do nothing, it becomes loose talk (see p. xx). Not only does it not have meaning; it's worse than that. It has counter-meaning, and it squelches even your ability to imagine yourself carrying through on your word. Part X loves loose talk, as it destroys your confidence to take action.

The second tool for getting out of the Safety Zone is density, which is the number of times you take action. Density translates to the quantity of action steps you take—in a day, or in a week, or in an hour—to get out of the Safety Zone. These steps are almost mathematical in terms of success or failure. Some people might have one hundred times the density of action than someone else. You can think of this as a pre-win, which means the moment you take action before you even know what the result is going to be, you've already won. You've already won by the action itself, independently of how well you take the action or any exterior success. Just taking the action is winning.

Eating the "death cookie" is the third tool for getting out of the Safety Zone. Pick the hardest thing you can stand to do, not because you're going to get anything out of it right at the moment, but because it changes your awareness of yourself and what you're capable of. To change your life, you have to change your relationship to fear. Think of these opportunities to act in the face of fear as death cookies.

Phil's Story: Howard Benjamin and Speed

When I was a young psychiatrist, I did some work at a place called the Center for the Healing Arts, which offered free psychotherapy to cancer patients. I don't know if we accomplished much—there was a lot of self-congratulatory bullshit about our good work and some press, which drew the attention of this man named Howard Benjamin. Benjamin was a sixty-year-old real estate lawyer in Los Angeles who had become so rich he didn't want to work anymore. He walked into the Center for the Healing Arts and said, "I'm yours, and I'm rich—I have nothing but time, so tell me what to do." They told him to get lost because he didn't have the right credentials.

Benjamin had a big mouth and no apparent fear, and he came alive when he could go up against people. So he bought a building and started his own center for the healing arts—and recruited me and some of the other shrinks to help him. Every Tuesday, we would meet and brainstorm. Somebody would say, "There's a guy I trained under in Texas who has an interesting approach to fear," or "My cousin is working on a novel treatment for breast cancer." Benjamin's secretary sat in these meetings with a phone, and he'd make her make the call right then.

This *really* freaked me out. Normally, when you have to do something anxiety-provoking, you want to dull your anxiety by thinking it over. But he didn't do that: He took the action as soon as possible.

I found this terrifying and fascinating—it showed me a kind of wild-ness and willingness that hadn't been part of my upbringing. This was my first experience of what I would come to call "speed."

Dealing with Fear

You have to be able to tap into the same level that caused a problem in the first place, which, in this case, is fear. Behaviorally, you have to pick out a few things that scare the shit out of you. And you have to focus on them, not because you're trying to win or get a tremendous material outcome. But you're doing it to decondition yourself from fear.

When I was young, I was on the Staten Island Ferry with my friend David Goldwater's father, who was a lawyer. They would rope off many of the sections when the boat wasn't full with signs saying that you weren't allowed to cross. David Goldwater's father crossed every single rope. That was the first time I'd seen anything like that—it was terrifying, almost as if I had done it myself and they were going to come and get me. But he would not be con-strained or restrained by stupid rules. He never paused to process his fear. For him, progress was about how quickly he could take the next step.

Fear is the terror that comes when you think you might be forced out of the Safety Zone. Fear is so paralyzing for people that it makes you easy prey for Part X.

Part X's power over you comes from the idea that it can enable you to avoid whatever you fear. It says, *With my help, you can get through this; you don't have to do what makes you scared.* Part X has an infinite number of ways to convince you that you don't need to face what you fear or what scares you. These are false promises. In fact, Part X's favorite move is to give you a problem you don't need to have. Every time you encounter fear, use the "Reversal of Desire," which I will teach you in the section on Pain, the first domain (see p. 65).

Patient Story: Vietnam Vet

Early in my career, I had two patients who knew each other from Vietnam. One of them had become a prominent public figure; the other was a lawyer, a regular California guy. The regular California guy liked to talk about Vietnam—in fact, he's the only guy I've ever heard speak honestly about his experience. He told me how much he liked the war—and that he liked killing people. He would get this look in his eyes—sometimes you see it in cops—like an animal sizing you up before he eats you. Other than this, he looked like me, even though he had this other thing inside him. He would talk about Vietnam and killing people with no emotion at all—and notably, no fear. Then we started doing couples therapy with his girlfriend— they were arguing about whether they would get married. When he left sessions with her, he was so anxious and frightened, he would get flop sweat. He had no fear in the face of one of the world's greatest horrors and yet was scared shitless of his girlfriend. Fear holds people back because it's not rational—it's unpredictable and uncooperative and does not abide by logic.

Exercise: Where Part X Convinces You to Avoid Fear

Make a list of all three domains. Next, write down what Part X does in each domain to block your progress, how that comes out symptomatically, and the reward of finally being non-avoidant. Do this in every domain. Make a positive declaration: *The only way I can defeat the lies that Part X showers me with is to recognize Part X* (see the section on P.R.I.M., p. 35). Recognize that Part X is giving you a false vision of reality—the idea that you can develop yourself and find your potential without having to face your fears—and that this idea is ridiculous. It is a form of false magic. Think about where you are doing Part X's bidding and hanging out in the Safety Zone, and where you have convinced yourself that you can create alone, without calling in higher forces to help you.

CHAPTER 6

Domain 1: Pain

You Earn: Ability to Expand

Pain, in any context, always makes you feel as if something is wrong with you. Pain is conflated with death—the number one reason people avoid painful things is that they confuse pain with dying. They don't think they will survive. Stick with me. You need tools that allow you to go through this symbolic death test, so you realize that instead of dying, you're actually going to expand. If you know how to look at death properly, you realize that dying is experiencing.

The universe is not designed for your comfort. It is designed to support you by pushing you forward. This support from the universe is not the same thing as eliminating all pain. Pain is any event in which you meet the universe, and it hurts. It could be rejection, it could be failure, it could be loss, it could be encountering someone who comes onto you and acts badly. Put simply, pain is what you feel when you are not in harmony in the world and when the world is not receiving you in the way you would like.

Forget about avoiding pain. It's impossible. Yes, we'd all like to live in a congenial world, but that's just a fantasy. Also, when you attempt to avoid pain, you lose self-esteem, and self-esteem is essential for contending with life and realizing your potential. At its bare bones, the definition of self-esteem is your ability to expand your pain tolerance. Self-esteem does not come from having gone to the right junior high school or having a nice car. When we strip down the human experience to its most basic level, self-esteem is important because it shows you that you've gone through this before, that you've built faith in your own self-reliance. You're in a learning curve where you're constantly expanding your capacity for pain and discomfort. Your job in life is to keep this process going.

An increase in pain tolerance leads to an increase in confidence and self-esteem: We widen and deepen our capacity to deal with life. Courage is the ability to stay in the pain. As someone once said, real courage is staying in the game for a second longer than the others. Part X wants you to quit the game; that's its main goal. It encourages this by promising you something that doesn't exist, that you can never attain—because you haven't experienced or gotten it, you can't see your way forward to getting it in the future. You see no reason to keep living, as Part X has destroyed hope. The only antidote to this is to develop faith, which is the subject of the domain of Uncertainty (see p. 86).

When you use the tools to fight pain, you become a stronger ally for fighting the war and being a part of the world. It also makes you aware of yourself. You will learn how to do things that are uncomfortable, that you don't want to do, but you will feel compelled to do them anyway.

When we think of pain, we typically think primarily of physical trauma—getting punched in the face, delivering a baby, or breaking a bone in an accident. But emotional and psychological pain is often experienced as the same level of torment—or worse—than physical pain. While physical pain usually gets less and less intense over time, psychological pain usually increases, getting more and more intense. Physiologically, the body is geared toward healing physical pain, but not so with mental pain. In fact, mental pain can be kept running by Part X. You must pay equal or more attention to psychological pain because it will not go away by itself.

The purpose of the exercises in this section is to get you to understand what both types of pain feel like—and how to embrace them.

The Maze

The Chinese have a saying: Those consumed by revenge must have too much time on their hands. We enter the Maze when our feelings are hurt, or when we feel we've been mistreated, and we can't let go of the situation. As a result, there's no forward motion. We obsess and ruminate.

Let's say you're driving on the freeway, and you rear-end a guy. Because it's L.A., you're going three miles per hour, but you tap his car. You both get out and he goes nuts on you. You have some choices. You can't get back in your car and drive away because it's rush hour; you won't get very far. You can try to calm him down, you can apologize, or you can scream back. But none of these tactics will solve your problem if this guy gets into your mind. While physical pain resolves itself—a black eye will be better in a week—emotional pain is different. Emotional pain is the only kind of pain that can get worse as time goes on because your ego holds onto it. Part X says, *You must get recompense.* Nope. Fairness is the booby prize that's worth nothing. But the Maze convinces you otherwise.

The Maze appears when someone has injured you or treated you unfairly or owes you something and won't give it to you. You become fixated on them, and you think that if you can only get them to admit they've been unfair and get them to pay you back, you'll be free. But you know how that ends. The only way to get out of the Maze is not to win. The only way you can get out of it is to say, *I don't have enough time to waste on this shit, so I have to let the other guy win.* The moment you do this in your mind, you can move forward. Picture a corkscrew—that's the Maze that you're caught inside and can't get out. It just keeps going and going and going.

The Maze represents your posture, or your interpretation of life, when you say, *I've been wronged; it's not fair. The person who wronged* me—*robbed me, punched me in the face, disparaged me*—has to make up for that in some way. *I refuse to take even one more step in the direction of my goals and my needs until I get paid.* It is predicated on the idea that the universe is fair and is supposed to be fair. But if you're waiting for someone who has harmed or hurt you to apologize, you're an idiot.

In *Hamlet,* Prince Hamlet believes that the only way to restore the balance is to avenge his father's death. In other words: *I'm not leaving the Maze until I get paid.* Now, as you probably know, this didn't work out too well for Hamlet. Almost everybody in the play dies. You can see this so clearly in the modern world, where conflicts often end with two supreme assholes standing on either side, the rest of us almost unable to differentiate one from the other.

The tools are so important because they teach you how to mobilize or marshal a certain kind of force that only comes from the lower chakras. The third eye, which is part of the upper chakras, is more intellectual, whereas the solar plexus is lower and more sensate. Part X can take over both of them, but it really loves to take over your mind, when it says to you, *You were wronged.* When Part X is in control, it will have a different reaction to a narcissistic injury than someone who is more mature or reasonable. Part X insists to you that you need to get paid, and you know what you deserve. This may sound reasonable, but it's really saying that the person believes the world should look at the world through their eyes. It's actually a crazy idea: If I think this is unfair, everyone will see that it's unfair.

Everyone gets stuck in the Maze at some point. We all know people from childhood who are stuck in the Maze—when you see them again after thirty years, nothing has changed. They'll usually have some story to tell you about why. This is one reason it can be hard to maintain friendships over time: The Maze takes people away and prevents them from growing. They're stuck in the Maze and they're boring. They've collected all these trophies of narcissistic injuries where they feel they've been wronged, a trophy wall of booby prizes.

The more you work on yourself and pull yourself out of the Maze, the more Part X will shrink. It's not a miracle, but things start to slow down a little so you feel more capable of seeing it happen and catching yourself before you're stuck.

People are different, but I see two things happen that force people out of the Maze. The first is that they miss a tremendous opportunity, and they're pissed at themselves. The second is that they might meet someone who will influence them in a positive sense, and they'll pick up their worldview, where they'll start to understand that it doesn't matter how unfair the world is. You're better off saying, *I'm going to get up, go to work, and get fucked over, every day of the rest of my life.*

To get out of the Maze, you can use the strategy called Reversal of Desire (see p. 73), particularly if it's a narcissistic injury where you perceive that somebody has done something aggressive to you. You use Reversal of Desire to go right at the aggressive affront, and essentially say that you want the person to fuck you over even more.

And then there's "Active Love," which you send to the person who sent you into the Maze in the first place.

Tool: Active Love

Barry Michels and I wrote about Active Love and Reversal of Desire in *The Tools,* because they are basic and essential tools for almost any situation. Active Love works to get you out of the Maze incredibly well because you can look at love as a substance, just like water. You can think of it as a liquid substance that's always available to you, infinitely available to you.

So let's say Hitler is driving past my building. So long as I have a hose and water, a metaphor for Active Love, I could wash his car. I might not want to, but I could turn on the water and do this. If you can wash his car, you can send him Active Love. You're not held back, even though it's Hitler, because the tool itself is meant to be used in all situations. This is because it's not a tool that's about the person you're sending the Active Love to. It's a tool that makes *you* whole. Because if you won't submit to the consistent need to send love out to the world, if you make it conditional, *you* become injured by that. That's the irony. If you won't send Active Love, it means that you're withholding something. Obviously, you're withholding something from the person you're angry at, and perhaps they deserve it, but you're also withholding something from yourself. Human beings want to be in this expansive state. It's not a moral or philosophic idea; it's an instinct. If we're not in that giving state, we feel like shit, because we feel that something is missing. The ego tries to stop you from sending Active Love by saying, *Oh no, no way, I want to get paid first.* But the heart has an infinite amount of energy that it can just give away: Love is an infinite resource. And not only that, but the universe is moving forward and expanding, and you need to give love at the same pace. Do not be stingy.

1. The first step is called **Concentration**. You suck all the love in the universe into your chest.

2. The second step is called **Transmission**, when you send the love to the hated person.

3. The final step is called **Penetration**, which is the most important step. You don't just see the love as it's directed toward another person, you actually feel it. It's like riding a wave of love right into the other person. When it goes inside the other person, at that point, nothing is missing anymore. You are then home yourself, and you become less interested and less needy about what you'll get back from them. You've transcended them and are now functioning at a higher level. I call this spiritual physics.

These steps are so powerful, and yet so few people can really grasp them. It's worth noting that it can feel easier to send Active Love to Hitler than to your ex-husband because you didn't know Hitler, and it's not as personal. For your ex-husband, see "Systematic Injury" below.

Systematic Injury

Every human being has the impulse to express themselves in a way that connects them to another person. This is the structure of life. Think about Genesis, when God says, "*Let there be light.*" Nobody is around, theoretically. But for something to be real, there must be an audience. Connection and relationship is the source of life. So, if you hate someone—even momentarily—it's very hard to keep up that flowing attitude of self-expression. But when you refuse to really connect to the other person, you actually get weaker. It's like your being starts to attenuate and stretch out all over the place, and you are alone. If you refuse to say something or don't express yourself, you've failed in your responsibility to be a human being.

The best definition of a narcissist is someone who doesn't really know what you're thinking or feeling and has no intention of finding out, because you don't really exist as a human being to them. To exist as a human being requires you to express yourself to another person. Anything you say, including judgments, must be directed at another person, even if the other person doesn't exist. Otherwise it's not real. People don't like this. The reason they don't like this is because it's anti-narcissistic.

There are people in our lives whom we hate—often, they cause us to end up in the Maze (see p. 67). And because our hate is strong, it can feel impossible to generate love, particularly unconditional love for someone who systematically injures you. Injury is the absence of love; that's the opposite way to define it. You can recover from systematic injury so long as you accept that the recovery period never ends. It may feel impossible to produce love for this person, but if you can't do that, they will stay in your head forever and never leave. (Again, see "The Maze.")

If you think of love as an infinite, fluid substance, then by sending them love, you're not really letting this person off the hook. You're not saying that the systematic injury is okay; you're simply learning to make yourself whole despite this injury. Sure, your response to this person could be retaliation, hatred, or obsession—*or* it could be a great place to practice developing love in a situation where none of it comes naturally. People often think, *If I let this go, and I don't curse at this person and obsess about him, I'm going to lose touch with him.* If you can generate love when there's really no invitation to do this, even when you actively hate this person, then you're really free—and that's the best thing for the Life Force. Remember, the Life Force is a post-death force.

Sending love works (see "The Maze" and "Active Love"), but it is not a one-shot deal. You have to tell yourself, *I will go through this fucking exercise a million times. I don't care. I'm not going back to the way I lived before, because it sucked the highest parts of me and shed them on the ground.* As long as you won't accept that, you're stuck.

Phil's Story: The Running Back

When I was thirteen years old, I was in tenth grade. I was way ahead for my age, which meant I was scared out of my mind most of the time. It was the beginning of the year, and I was in a mechanical drawing class, also called drafting. This guy who looked like a gorilla sat next to me. He easily could have been seven years older than me—he definitely outweighed me by eighty pounds. He was the star running back for the Stuyvesant High School football team, which at the time was a very good team.

Neither of us could draft for shit. I was terrified to talk to him, but then he started to talk to me as he realized neither of us could draw properly and weren't going to get much out of the class. The only thing he wanted to talk about was football. Soon he opened up to me, and he told me that people criticized him, even though he was the best running back in high school football.

"It's not because I'm the fastest," he explained. "It's not because I have the best moves. But I am the best running back, better than all the other running backs if you look at the results. Here's what I do: When the linebacker comes in to tackle me, I make no effort to avoid them. I just stand there and let them smash me and we both get knocked to the ground. Then I pop up fast, while the other guy is still feeling woozy. It makes me feel like God."

He told me this about ten times, and every time, I thought to myself, *If I could get that degree of aggression and courage, I could do anything.* I forgot about it, but maybe ten years later, the story popped back into my mind, and I decided to try it. It worked right away. I called it the "law of fear," and it says that if you find yourself afraid of anything, anything at all, you have to go toward it. Ultimately, this became the basis of the Reversal of Desire.

Tool: Reversal of Desire

Because physical pain is concrete—and often temporary—it's the best training ground for working with the reality, and hidden gifts, of pain. Whenever I go to the dentist, for example, I use Reversal of Desire (ROD) the moment before the dentist begins to drill. You can use this tool any time—right before you act, at the moment of action, or on free-floating fears. It doesn't need to be tethered to a specific time or place.

1. Face the Pain
See the pain you are avoiding as a cloud in front of you. Silently scream, "Bring it on!"

2. Move Toward the Pain
Silently scream, "I love pain!" while you keep moving forward into the cloud. Embrace the pain so deeply that you become one with it.

3. Freedom
Feel the cloud spit you out and close behind you. Say inwardly, "Pain sets me free!" As you leave the cloud, feel yourself propelled forward into a realm of pure light.

Exercise: Practicing Reversal of Desire

Find one opportunity a day to practice Reversal of Desire: Start with something pedestrian in the World of Small Things that requires physical action, like a phone call you've been putting off or a trip to the dry cleaners. Once you understand what the tool feels like in your body—the way it makes you feel alive and in motion—graduate to more complex tasks that you've been avoiding, resisting, or putting off. Often, my patients take too big of a bite and are immediately defeated and discouraged—this is why I bring them back to the Life Force and the World of Small Things. If you want to write a book but have been avoiding this for a decade, you cannot use Reversal of Desire once to force yourself to sit down and write ninety thousand words. That's too much pain at once. This isn't about a single victory; this is about building an ongoing relationship with the universe, of seeing creation as a verb. You use Reversal of Desire to write two hundred words. And then you use it again.

Patient Story: The Marlboro Man

This guy I know was an assistant director on a Marlboro Man commercial. For some reason, they were shooting it on the water in those pencil boats that go really fast. Anyway, they were up north and it was really cold—they were fucking around in the boats, and somebody fell out. The water was so cold—you can only live in water like that briefly, maybe five minutes. The crew was screaming and everyone was going crazy, but the Marlboro Man kept his cool.

He saw what was going on, and instead of going right to the person who was basically drowning and dying, he started to circle him—if he had driven right at him with the boat, he would have killed him, but everyone had lost their minds, and they didn't know what he was doing. The crew was getting more and more crazed as the circles got smaller and smaller. Finally, he reached the guy, and instead of just dragging him out of the water, he dipped him under water. About three seconds later, he popped up—the Marlboro Man grabbed him and pulled him into the boat.

Everyone's instinct was to get this guy out of pain as fast as possible, but the Marlboro Man realized that there was a process: You have to go through the pain before you can bounce out of it.

Tool: Pain Chambers

SMALL CHAMBER: The pain is fully spilled out, flooding your psyche.

MEDIUM CHAMBER: The pain is spilling out; you can't handle it.

LARGE CHAMBER: The pain reaches the point where it could spill out but doesn't.

EACH TIME YOU TOLERATE THE SPILLING THE CHAMBER GETS BIGGER

THE CHAMBERS

We want to increase our capacity for pain. Pain spills over if you have a very small chamber for tolerating or holding it. This creates a chaotic effect in people's emotional lives—and the people around them. If the chamber gets bigger, slowly, it can contain more of the pain without spilling over. The pain doesn't go away; you just build your capacity to hold it in, without letting it make you lose control of your emotions or make bad decisions. The pain is still there, but your chamber is bigger.

When you can't contain pain, then you either become compulsive (drugs, alcohol, rage, etc.), or you run away from the playing field. But the real question is how do you grow from the little chamber to the much bigger one? This is important because the bigger one reminds you that you've done this before and you can tolerate it.

We've illustrated three chambers here, but there could be three hundred of them.

To make the chamber bigger, metaphorically, you need to die. If you're reading this and thinking, *There are a lot of positive things happening in my life that challenge me, and so my pain chambers will get bigger as a result, because I'm going to make pain my friend,* you should know it doesn't work like that. There's a little death between every leap in an expansion of your pain chamber. The death is to your ego, and this is what confuses people. Death is whatever is beyond what you thought you could survive.

When I first started speaking in public, I'd begin to shake. I was terrified. So, I decided to see public speaking as a death. I would imagine it as a circle that symbolized death—a "death cookie." I understood that if I ate this death cookie, it would transform me. If I spit it out, if I left the scene of the crime, I'd get nothing except for the pain. The death cookie is the metaphor for fully accepting the fear and pain of something so that you can move forward. It's a waste of time to stop being afraid—you can be as scared as you want, just stop avoiding taking action. The death cookie doesn't have to have value. It's enough for the death cookie to represent symbolic death: You want to eat as many of them as you can.

Phil's Story: Boxing Gym

When I was about twenty-six, I was so afraid of getting beaten up that I decided to take up boxing. I trained at a gym on Willis Avenue, in the heart of the South Bronx. The neighborhood was so bad that sometimes you'd walk two or three blocks, and everything would be leveled. There was a guy living in the rubble who even had a goat. I was the only white guy who trained at this gym, which was a very macho environment. There was one guy there, a professional boxer, who would always beat me up. We'd spar, and he'd beat the shit out of me. I would say to myself, *This guy really hates me.* We never spoke.

I had this little forest green Triumph Spitfire, a tiny car, that I'd park outside of the gym. One night, as I climbed in, I realized that someone had been inside—all the wires were pulled out. I had one thought: *I'm dead.* It was dark out, there was no way I could drive the car, and it was a notoriously dangerous neighborhood. Suddenly, a guy stepped out of the shadows—the boxer from the gym. So, I thought again: *I'm dead.* But he started talking to me and reassuring me. He told me he would take care of it, that his cousin owned a garage nearby. He walked me to the subway so I could get the hell out of there. I was stunned. Later on, I realized that you're living a metaphor in the gym, going through a rite of passage. They didn't care that I was white. That I was willing to go up there three times a week and get hit in the face—that I was willing to eat the death cookie—meant that I was accepted. The feeling was actually very loving. This confused me for a long time, though I understand it now perfectly. If you go through something that incites fear in you with someone else, and if you don't run away, you change the relationship. In past eras, they called this "initiation." The boxing community saw that I was willing to go through death, again and again.

Sometimes physical pain is easier for us to imagine—and people try to get really good at contending with pain by building physical strength. But this is psychological death. Similar symbolic deaths might be the loss of a job, or an opportunity, or a relationship, or a loved one. A door to you closes. But the more you can think of this as a dynamic process for looking at death, the more it will help you—even to the extent of helping you with real, physical death.

Exercise: Life Review

Starting with today and working backwards, plot out the pain points in your life and where you have gotten bigger as a result.

What have you survived that felt unsurvivable?

Draw your pain chambers as they relate to how you've been pushed to expand and grow.

Patient Story: Medication-Free Birth

One of my patients decided to have a medication-free birth at a birthing center. She spent many hours in labor and nothing happened. She told me how she was scared, and in pain, and became convinced that she couldn't do it and wanted to go to the hospital. But as she was making the call, she thought about the pain chambers.

"I kept reminding myself my body was designed to do this, and this is not the worst of it! With every worse contraction, I killed the part of me that couldn't, and then I could. I died a thousand deaths over the course of forty-six hours of labor . . . and my pain chamber became very large."

Higher Bond

If you look at the picture of a relationship, it's not a schematic of two stick figures fighting against each other. If it's a healthy dynamic, let's say in a marriage, what you should see is an overlap here, which I call the "higher bond." It's a third entity in the relationship. If there were just two people in a relationship—I insult you and you insult me

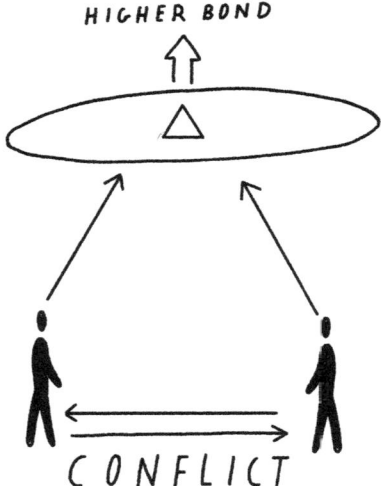

back—there would be very little leeway for movement, and very little power in the dynamic. But that third part, the higher bond, which is the top of the pyramid, is the level at which you want to solve the problem.

This is hard, because each person's Part X is looking at the other person and saying, *How can I fuck them up and draw them back down into the morass of their feelings and victimization?* But the remedy to this is not face-to-face. It's up here, in this higher bond. If somebody hurts your feelings, the first thought you should have is not *How do I get revenge?* or *How do I get them to admit that they treated me badly?* That's a waste of time and doesn't work. That's a repetitive, fruitless, egotistical attempt to be treated fairly. And ironically, the result of being in this state is that you are never treated fairly. At the moment of injury, you might even turn to your partner and say, "I wouldn't feel so injured if you weren't such an asshole," or "I wouldn't be so upset if you paid more attention to me." But even those words really won't make a difference. You are still searching for a solution on the lower level, the personal level.

Pain itself is a narcissistic injury, because Part X tells you that you should be sanctioned for being a bad boy or girl. Someone attacks you, and you feel that it's your own fault that they attacked you, that you deserve it. And the pathway to experiencing a higher bond seems out of reach.

The higher bond is infused with higher forces, and it seeks to solve conflict on a different level, a level that is relatively selfless and not willing to quit under any circumstance.

The higher bond doesn't have the qualities of A versus B, or winner and loser; competition is very lower bond, which is limiting. As long as people think they can win, and that they can select a route to defeat the other person, we are in trouble. The only way a relationship can survive is for both parties to repent. This means restraining all the impulses that drag you into the lower, material world. People don't like this because they think they will be giving up a prize. It creates a violent counterreaction because you don't get a prize—when you enter a higher bond, you're not even close to a prize. A higher bond is Universe Two; the lower bond is Universe One, where you want to get yours, where it's transactional. In the lower bond, love, attention, and ideas are given with a limitation. The opposite of this—the higher bond—has access to complete abundance.

The higher bond gives without constraint. The lower bond is a game of musical chairs where everybody loses. The higher bond is a field created by two people who have to transcend the lower bond. In the higher bond, you can't just take—you also have to give something to the world.

In a spiritual sense, one organ in our body has access to limitless energy. The heart is the one that must attend to the rift in this relationship. The heart is connected to higher forces that are infinite. It's the only organ in the body that has this type of connection. Every parent knows this feeling, a feeling of infinite energy that comes from the heart instead of the brain, already there in infinite supply without having to do anything. The ego doesn't like that.

Courage is also relevant here. How could it be that the loving forces, and the courageous parts of you, are both coming from the heart? Love and courage go together, which makes intuitive sense, but people don't really have a way to explain this to themselves. You can give away as much love as you want, and you will end with the same amount, if not more, than you had before. Courage is the exact same—you don't use it up. The only other quality that is infinite in this way is creativity, which is connected to the Life Force. I call the tool for love "overflow": I love you because I have so much love to give, I can give it all to you without any dent—I have endless, infinite resources. Courage is the same. The equivalent of Active Love for courage is infinite life: I'm not afraid; you can even kill me, but it won't make any difference. My Life Force is infinite.

Patient Story: D

One of my patients, whom we'll call D, was dealing with cardiovascular problems. His doctor had ordered him to get on the treadmill every day. But he didn't want to. We started by introducing him to his Life Force (see p. 9) in the World of Small Things (see p. 15). I made him add one minute to his time on the treadmill every day. Slowly, he got from about ninety seconds to twenty minutes. With every minute that he added, the belief that he couldn't died, and then . . . he did.

While he had to push through a lot of resistance on the treadmill, he had no resistance to prostitutes. He was addicted to hookers. An addict does not want to go through the first type of pain, which is the pain of getting sober. Yet counterintuitively, the addict will have no problem dealing with the other kind of pain, which is getting to the next dose or dealing with a horrendous hangover or other negative repercussions in their life. The first kind of pain requires forward motion, whereas the second kind of pain is fueled by Part X's desire to keep you right where you are.

Someone with an active addiction has no interest in, or even awareness of, the future—even though the future's going to happen in ten minutes when he'll be sick again and want another fix. It's like that doesn't exist. The only thing that exists is the gratification and the imagined bliss. This is the Realm of Illusion, which says, *You're going to get this without really doing anything.*

It doesn't have to be heroin—it could be food, or a relentless and obsessive desire for a part in a play, or really anything that feels compulsive where there seems to exist a pantheistic solution to all of your problems. You'll get the thing and all will be well. But really, we're talking about expectations that are impossible to meet or experience.

Dynamic Inversion

Impulses travel through your lower channel. If you block an impulse, it goes back inside in a process called inversion. This isn't about depriving yourself, which is how most people interpret the action. It's a dynamic inversion because, as in chemistry, the impulse moves up to your heart and comes out through the higher channel. The higher channel is different from the lower channel—it has a facility that the lower channel doesn't have. The lower channel is stupid and operates on pure instinct, which usually causes disaster. But

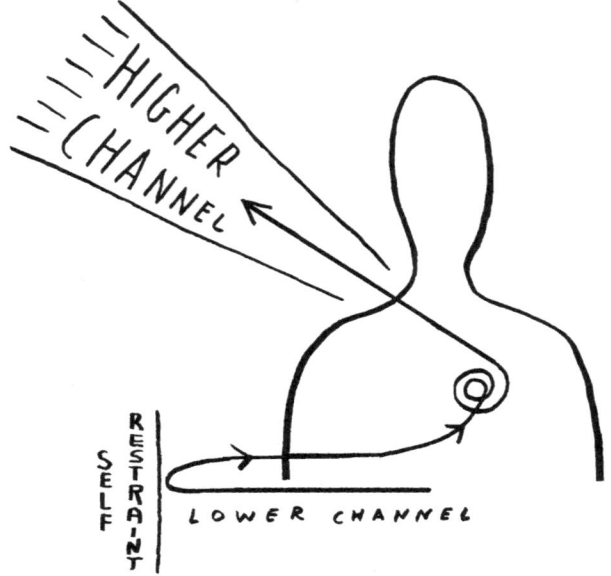

when the higher channel gets involved, it can join forces with other streams of energy. The stupidly desirous impulse gets reborn as something that's not selfish.

Patient Story: Coke Addict

My first or second patient in California was addicted to cocaine. This was California in the 1980s, so none of this was very earth-shattering, but she'd come to her sessions with a little vial of coke. She thought she was very cool, and she loved to criticize me for calling attention to the cocaine: *Are you some kind of sissy?*

I kept telling her that the drugs were not innocuous, that her bad habits were going to create problems for her. Eventually, I told her that I wouldn't treat her if she was doing blow, and to call me when she was off cocaine or had a reasonable plan for stopping. The next day, she was stoned, her car rolled down an embankment, and she ended up in the hospital. She was fine, but the doctor told her if she suffered another spinal injury, she'd be paralyzed. So she came back to therapy.

For someone like her, it was about self-restraint: If you can't restrain yourself in all things—not just what you're addicted to—and if you can't submit to discipline, it becomes impossible to control yourself. You have to do work in the World of Small Things, as it gives you an opportunity to practice being right in the moment and controlling your impulses. Any addiction, or anything you do that's unrestrained and undisciplined, makes your ego stronger. To control an impulse, you have to be in the moment and pay attention—if you don't do this, the impulse of Part X takes you over. Exercising self-restraint gives you entrée into a higher world. The lower world, simply because it's addictive, holds you in the lower world.

Tool: Hidden Resources

Most people dedicate their lives to never testing what they're capable of. This is why I try to push patients—and am trying to push you. I'm not going to push you far—consider it from Manhattan to Jersey. It's not a big step, but the willingness to take any step at all—with no guarantee of outcome—will become part of your identity. You can use past experiences to practice this skill, instead of waiting for new psychological deaths to happen. I want you to practice, because the highest and most human inner state occurs after there's been a disaster. Whether it's a failure on your part or a literal earthquake, it doesn't matter. You've been stripped bare. The universe wants you like that. Making any effort after the universe has forced you to fail is a bit like converting a little piece of rock. You can continue to do this, even on events from the past, by putting yourself back there. Or use it on an event from the present. I'm going to describe Position One and Position Two to you—both positions are a refusal to submit to the laws of reality.

Close your eyes and visualize that you are in **Position One,** where the Realm of Illusion doesn't exist and this all seems real. There are no penalties. If I get this thing, I'm safe, and everything is great.

Next, you're in **Position Two,** where you're getting the first inkling that this thing you thought would be great—a drug, the role in the play, a significant other—isn't working for you.

Then, imagine that you're rolling down a hill on your ass—pick out the bottom line, **Position Three,** where you will finally stop rolling because you've hit the lowest possible point. At this level, everything in life has failed you. Really feel this and put yourself inside this moment—be inside your own bloodstream.

Finally, put yourself in a **historical position**—it could be yesterday, it could be in junior high—where you didn't have any control in one of these types of situations. You're taking the worst experiences from your past, packaging them, and then training yourself to evoke them so that you can practice experiencing reality, no matter how unpleasant it is. By doing this, you are creating a change that could go on for the rest of your life. Your goal is to create the tiniest, smallest emotional accomplishment by reexperiencing your painful realities. And you're going to do it over and over again.

Even though this may not be pleasant and may hurt you, you are doing something important: You're creating meaning. Just as expanding your pain chambers increases self-esteem, this makes your life become meaningful and expands your ability to experience reality.

Tool: Loss Processing

The ability to process loss, which is a type of death, is probably the most creative skill you can develop. Tolerating loss is not the same thing as succeeding, but it contains something that's very important. If you lose one thing, like money, that's not so good. But if you lose everything, you get a bonus, which is entrée into a different world. I call this the Sun World, a world of pure creativity.

For the purpose of this exercise, think of something that you absolutely don't want to lose. Imagine you're hanging from the trunk of a tree that's sticking out, and you're afraid you're going to get pushed off the ledge. At that point, you'll lose whatever it is you don't want to lose. So let go and begin to fall gently, not fast. Below you, you'll see that you're falling into a sun. This is much less scary than you would think. Now, as you are on the way down, you say, "I'm willing to lose everything." The moment you say it, you hit the sun's surface; you feel your body giving way. Without a body, you don't have anything, at least not in Universe One.

Even though you don't have a physical body—you burn up when you hit the Sun World—and can't take physical possession of anything, what you do have is a new, different world. When you look around, you have a vision of yourself, outflowing, pure love and creativity in all directions, holding nothing back. You're just pure sun radiating from every point in the universe. You are everywhere.

You want to do this fast, as one flowing experience. My patients frequently tell me that they envision themselves as falling backwards, with their arms extended. I don't know why that's the pattern—I could make something up about how there's some primate part of us that recalls falling out of trees like this—but this is the pattern. It might be because it most fully encapsulates the image of letting go—of letting go of the attachments and objects that define Universe One and realizing that you actually can live without them.

CHAPTER 7

Domain 2: Uncertainty

You Earn: Ability to Have Faith

The universe is in constant flux, constant motion. Everything is changing every second. Reality, which is most accurately represented by Universe Two, is not like the material world or Universe One, where you can hang your hat on Marxism or an Academy Award. There's nothing like that in the real universe. In this greater reality, the only stability you have, the only real victory that you can have, is over your inner state. While the outer state is unpredictable, the inner state can be approached in a way that helps you rather than hurts you. It's not about "controlling" the inner state, but more about gently managing it.

The universe is chaotic in and of itself. There's no way any human being could be privy to what will happen next. It's not a bad thing that we're not privy to the rules of the universe, because knowing what will happen will not solve our anxiety—it would actually be crippling. If you want absolute security, which I call cosmic safety, you end up instead with cosmic terror, what I call the cosmic twins. You can't belie this truth; it's a law of spiritual physics. If the world were predictable, you'd be paralyzed from moving forward.

To deal with uncertainty, you must deal with reality. Our entire society is designed to keep you away from reality: In fact, most of us are convinced that luck or some magical practice or some divine intervention will get us off the hook of dealing with these three undeniable realities, these three domains. But as I've established, you cannot survive long in the Realm of Illusion. There is no cure for uncertainty: Working with reality requires taking action and making choices without proof.

So, what is the right way to perceive or understand the world? It has to be through sensation. That's the trickiest part. This uncertain world can only be perceived in sensation—you can feel the world, but you can't understand it. It happens on the instinctual level, not the intellectual level. To feel the world, you must work on your intuition—that's where your sensations work to guide you forward. Most people waste their lives trying to "figure it out." Embracing the domain of uncertainty requires saying, *What I'm really doing here is not trying to get any result at all; I'm just trying to change my state of mind and my habits.* You must consider that this shift is the highest value, not what happens. The nonverbal part of us can feel reality— you must have faith that this feeling organ is somehow hooked up with your karma.

In a world that's becoming more data rich and AI-centric, people are paralyzed from making their own decisions. We're giving data sets to machines to make decisions for us. In Universe One, we want to pretend we can mathematicize a decision so it's no longer a decision. It is not that different from my father joining the Communist Party because he thought that it could predict what was going to happen. (He was exactly wrong, by the way.)

You must continue to engage with no guarantee of outcome. To that end, it may seem obvious, but voting in an election makes a difference. I used to say to myself when I was in my thirties and busy as a doctor, *I'm happy to make a difference, but no one has ever won and lost an election by one vote. So I'm not going to vote today, because I want to work, or I want to go to the beach.* But that's wrong. You're denying the significance of taking action. An election is won numerically, so it seems like something from Universe One, but in reality, when you cast your vote, you are stamping your vision and your willingness to sacrifice with no guarantees of any outcome on the back of an envelope. You need an entire culture that understands and develops this vision. Because this is the faith that can defeat evil—a belief in taking action regardless of the outcome.

If you only take one thing from this entire book, I hope it's this: **The most important tool for contending with life is freely chosen faith.** This faith is "chosen" for no other reason than your desire to have faith. To deal with reality, you must accept the fact that reality is unpredictable and that you must act anyway, using only the faith that you've chosen to have.

Demanding Proof: Good vs. Evil Wedding Cakes

The Good Wedding Cake
Confidence is built on **action**, which relies on . . . **faith**. This faith is *freely chosen* and will feel like an irrational choice. This is the only way to stay connected to the universe, and it's delicious.

The Evil Wedding Cake
Egotism insists on **proof** of its correctness, which rests on the presence of **doubt**. This is a shit cake and a terrible way to live: You either end up as a know-it-all or you're mostly wrong.

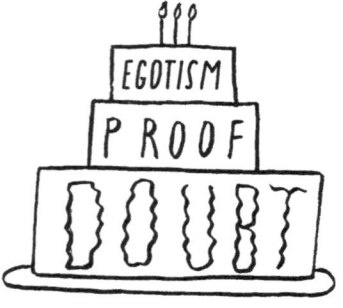

THE WEDDING CAKES are two of the most important pyramids in my system. Weddings and marriage are symbolically relevant. Carl Jung would often talk about the inner marriage of the masculine and the feminine—the union of two forces makes a third. The evil wedding cake represents Universe One, while the good wedding cake represents Universe Two.

The foundational level of the evil wedding cake is doubt, which consumes the average person. They say, "I doubt everything until proven otherwise. If you present me with proof, then I can overcome doubt." The only time and place where this model of doubt and proof makes sense is when you are a scientist doing an experiment in a lab. In every other context, the need to have proof before you will stop doubting everything sucks. In this worldview, the only two possible outcomes are being absolutely right, the smartest person in the world, or absolutely wrong, not knowing shit. The whole concept is bullshit. If you have no faith and choose to accept only the evidence that comes from pure materialism, you are completely limited by your need for proof. That's why the base layer of the evil wedding cake is doubt, which rejects everything unless it can be proven.

When you live in Universe One, you are choosing to live in the realm of the evil wedding cake—here, you start to let your doubts seek out and make decisions for you. You try to rely on the idea that you are *a keen observer and can prove everything mathematically,* which is based on doubt. It takes you away from reality and doesn't help you. Part X wants you to eat the evil wedding cake. The only remedy is to eat the good wedding cake instead.

Faith, which is the base layer of the good wedding cake, is the antidote to Part X, because only faith allows you to live in Universe Two, a universe that means something (see p. 40).

Symbolically, a wedding cake is a union of two opposing forces. And the outcome of the first two layers (faith plus action) is the top layer of the good wedding cake—confidence. Confidence has nothing to do with results. Confidence is not the product of a cognitive victory—this value is only granted to people who are in process, independent of the results. Confidence is the product of a lower, non-logical, impossible-to-prove way of looking at the world, which is faith. And the only way you can tap into faith is to choose it, to do it for no reason. This drives people nuts, but I find that people who live through this process end up being much stronger, and as a side effect, much better decision-makers.

In order to work with faith, you are not looking for results or outcomes—you are working with faith to strengthen your intuition. Confidence is a good proxy for the feeling that comes from strong intuition. And strong intuition only comes from taking a lot of turns at bat. A singular victory or failure means nothing.

To get faith, you have to practice. Faith is a muscle memory of a state that you can return to at will. Faith is higher than logic, and thus can't be proven by logic. Plus, people who think they're doing everything logically are idiots. Most of the action in the world is not arranged. You can arrange your habits, but you can't arrange the results.

The only thing you can control is your inner state; you can't control the outcome. Controlling the outcome is impossible. But you can become confident in yourself that you're going to use this model no matter what. If you don't have faith, you will never get confidence, because you can't look for confidence outside yourself. Confidence must come from the foundation of faith, a faith that's completely irrational and unprovable. Faith doesn't come because you've "figured it out."

To have faith, you have to take action in the dark—you have to give yourself completely over to the recognition that *you know nothing and are going to take action anyway.* Within this reality, nothing is going to be fully proven or understood. Within this reality, God gives you permission to have faith for no reason.

Phil's Story: My Father and Joe

My father was a brilliant salesman, but he was never successful. The reason for this was simple: He was partnered with a guy named Joe who stole from him. Everybody liked my father, but everybody hated Joe. He was the sort of guy who would wear a purple shirt and a fancy suit and coat. I would ask my dad, "*Why don't we live like that?*" My father could have been very successful, and he could have made a lot of money, but he couldn't leave Joe. He wanted to get away from him, but he never could. He couldn't do it because he needed a guarantee from the universe that it would work out. He needed certainty. I was in my twenties when their business finally blasted off. My dad died ninety days later, at age sixty-six, still attached to this guy because he was "safe." The reason he felt safe was because my father knew he was smarter than Joe. He felt as though he had control in their relationship. He got to stay in the Safety Zone (see p. 59), and in his version of certainty—that Joe was a thief and a schmuck, and that he could do so much better without him, without ever doing anything about it and finding out. The price he paid for this version of safety was the complete loss of his freedom.

The Science of Reality

You need a procedure or protocol to judge whether you are building confidence for the pursuit of the good, or whether you are pursuing evil. In other words, you need what I call a "science of reality" which records your observations and predictions at every step of the process. There are evil forces that take humanity away from humans—this is the twisted drive of Part X—and so making Part X's drive conscious is necessary. The fact that you have to make that discrimination or identification without any guarantee that you're getting it right is a key element in these observations. We're not looking for being right all the time, but for the willingness to be wrong, for the awareness that you can't predict the future, though Part X will try to convince you that it can.

New patients would always say to me: "You can't prove this works; this is a fairy tale." My response was to never argue with them, never. I would say, "I have no opinion on that. But do what I tell you, use the tools, and if they don't move you forward, or give you better control of your impulses, fire me. In fact, I insist that you fire me." Strategically, this was very helpful because I was feeding back to the other person my belief that the value is always invisible. The results may be visible, but they are not the main value of living this way.

Exercise: Part X Predictions

In life, we must embrace a kind of ignorance (see p. 111)—we must accept that we will never know if we are doing well or not. The point is to continue to choose to do good things in the face of no proof. Part X will try to convince you that it knows the future. The point of the science of reality is to write down your predictions so that they're right in front of your face, and you can't deny that they are what you thought. Then you can't deny that 75 percent of the time, you are wrong.

When I was twenty-nine or thirty years old, I had a lot of patients, but I always thought, *I'm too young. I'm going to lose all my patients. Why would they want to pay me?* I started writing these Part X predictions down with the date and time on index cards at my desk. Usually I would wait for ten days or two weeks before looking again and weighing my predictions against what had happened. These cards were like real Valium: They helped reduce a lot of my worry about the future.

Make sure that you write your predictions down—you must do this so you can't be biased. Most people, once they have a problem and they solve it, don't want to think about the problem again. This gives Part X a tremendous leg up—so instead of making this a mental game, write it down. And don't congratulate yourself: Part X will keep raising the stakes and raising the stakes again. You want to make yourself into a passive observer in the face of Part X claiming to have a lock on the future, a future that is going to be bad. You can't fight that off by saying, *No, you're wrong, my future will be great.* You say instead, *I'm going to write down everything you predict, Part X, and we will look at those predictions together.* Get Part X's ruminations out of your head and onto a piece of paper.

1. Close your eyes and think of something in the future that scares you, or that you're worried might happen.

2. Write down the Part X predictions. Write down everything you expect to happen as a result of whatever it is that scares you.

3. In a couple of weeks, read your predictions to see if any of this stuff really happened.

4. Sometimes Part X will be right; often Part X will be wrong. The point is not to convince yourself to be certain that Part X is always wrong, but to reveal that you don't know, and that Part X certainly doesn't know, what's going to happen. This exercise illustrates that you're trying to create proof—part of the evil wedding cake—in a world where you truly need faith, faith freely and irrationally chosen.

The Intelligence of the Will and the Donut Shop

Your will itself is a sense organ—it's nonverbal, but it's very confident. In the ancient world, life was easier, because there was less cognition coming from the head. Most people couldn't even read. They were like guided missiles—pure sense organs who were *willing*. They were part of a collective, which pleased God. But everything changed as the world changed—people stopped relying solely on that state of being. Nobody cared to develop it anymore because they had telescopes and toilet bowls and other pieces of technology that changed their perception of the world. Once the printing press emerged, people had a voice. Ultimately, these anachronistic sense organs had to be upgraded—starting in about the year 1500, God upgraded the model, because the human race was craving and demanding a sense of meaning. This is when more cognitive skills came online, when *thinking* joined *willing* and *feeling*. Ultimately, God constructed the universe to force humans into the three domains, to force humans to stop avoiding. These three domains in aggregate represent the entire face of God, the simultaneous concurrence of these three ways of encountering the world. Each topography is like a piece of land that you own, that in total comprises the wholeness. But I don't want you to take my word for this, or for you to treat this book like "proof," as the whole point is that you need to proceed on faith, freely chosen.

Now, let's say you want to open a donut shop—that takes personal will. You would never undertake such an endeavor with just your mind, but the "intelligence of the will" prompts you to move forward—and the universe responds by giving you at least some of the things that you need to know.

Now, you could spend hours, days, and years reading about donut shops, going to business seminars and taking marketing classes to try to figure out how many glazed, sprinkled, and chocolate donuts to bake. I see this with my patients all the time: They want to create something, but they want to create it with built-in certainty of its success. People very much want this to be a cognitive process that can be solved. But you'll never figure it out until you actually just *open the donut shop*. It's only then will you discover what you need to know, only when you are right in the middle of the experience—in the process, you'll find your instincts. When you open the donut shop, instead of talking about it, or studying it, you actually trigger the Life Force.

In the first fifteen minutes of having your donut shop's doors open, you'll learn more about donut flavors and the intricacies of operating a shop than in fifteen years of research—and you'll be far more confident in what you're learning. Research isn't bad per se, but you'll never trust research because it hasn't been lived—it doesn't give you the right kind of information. Things will never work out the way you were planning for them to work out. On the other hand, the intelligence of the will is nonintellectual and comes through action—it will find you and give you what you need. Putting yourself in the center of the dynamic forces that control the universe is the intelligence of the will.

Patient Story: The Jewish Golfer

A Jewish golfer came to see me. There are really only two levels in professional golf: the players on the PGA Tour and everyone else. Well, this Jewish golfer was the best player in the developmental level right below the PGA—everyone would agree with that. But he could never quite earn enough points to break into the Tour. He would always be winning, and then would get to the sixteenth hole and fall apart—he'd shoot a twelve instead of a three or four and blow his score.

Now, I knew why he was failing, and it wasn't because he was a loser. I went into this really carefully with him to show him the decision he himself was making on the golf course. As we went into the process, it became clear that he knew, but could never admit it to himself.

I asked him one question: "Put yourself back at the sixteenth hole. When you fail and shoot a twelve instead of a four, how do you feel?"

Do you know what he answered? He said, "I feel good."

He felt relieved, because he couldn't tolerate the uncertainty. Ensuring he failed took the uncertainty out of the situation. He would rather shoot a nineteen and get it over with. This happens to all of us, all the time, on more subtle levels. It is very common.

We don't like to function in Universe One—we hate that it's competitive and exacting and limited and has a lot of nastiness—but we don't know the alternative. We end up in Universe One because we convince ourselves that it's certain.

Tool: The Instinct Cycle

The instinct cycle is a tool to train someone to trust their instincts, because when you're in uncertainty, that's all you have. This is how you function when you don't have the information—and quite frankly, you never have the information. An ability to tolerate consequences and recover is the only certainty you can have. This is why the string of pearls (see p. 111) is important: Identity can't be attached to whether you're going to win or lose. Simply, it's the process of activating your instinct cycle and knowing you're going to have to take the consequences—not only knowing this, but feeling good about this.

The instinct cycle is where you develop your intuition. It is an exercise that requires a committed and proactive willingness to be wrong. It's not the person who is right the most times who is the most confident, or who trusts the universe more completely—it's the person who works the cycle the most times. People always ask me, *"Well, if there's no logic to it to begin with, what's the advantage of repeating it over and over?"* And the answer is in its cyclicity: You're giving your unconscious room to draw its conclusions. It's like playing an instrument. You get better at it because it's a repetitive action; it's not coming from an intellectual process.

The key to the instinct cycle is that you accept the final step, which is the consequences. You will develop instinctual confidence, which means you're confident not because of any singular thing, but because of how you conduct yourself. It's very hard in our culture, almost impossible, to keep up our instincts, because we deny that everything is changing every second. Even if you're right once or twice, it makes no difference. You have to be in the process of continuing to take action in an environment where a lot of times, the consequence isn't going to be good. But if you can tolerate the consequences, even consequences you fear, you become unstoppable.

Refer back to "The Tents" (see p. 19): When you go off the path and hit a moment of truth, every time you go back on your path, you're creating a little bit of faith. The faith really comes from you showing up and taking action. The point is, the more that you can do that, and the less proof you need to get started, the better your intuition becomes.

The instinct cycle is simply a model for you to force yourself to make a lot of decisions and choices rapidly—many of these will be "wrong," but it doesn't matter. The person who wins, who develops the strongest intuition, is the person who works the cycle, not the person who is "right" the most number of times. Human beings are forced to contend with the inevitability of the world. Its value comes from the very awareness that there is no single escape from the unavoidable uncertainty that marks every human life. Contending with uncertainty is about a lifetime of dealing with insecurity—you can call it an adult religion, where the only thing that will help you is faith, freely chosen.

If you make your decisions based on the illusion that you can get it "right" and that there's a winner, you're dead. I used to treat a lot of high-level executives. These executives don't actually work all day. Really, all they do is make decisions. And the good ones know that they don't have enough information to make decisions logically—they must use their intuition and go on their gut. Your entire ability to work with uncertainty is to develop a force in you that transcends results, and in a sense, it transcends what you think you deserve or what you think you're trying to will into being by making a decision. This is where you get the power to create. The real power to create, and the hidden potential of all human beings, is by paying at the door of each of these domains and going through them. You must gain the ability to make decisions and create in spite of doubt. Another way to say this is that you will gain confidence in the face of doubt. Don't bullshit me, and don't bullshit yourself.

Indecision is one such impediment, or stalling tactic, to stop people from moving forward. People would come into my practice and ask, "*Do I buy this house or not? I might not be able to make my mortgage payments.*" But it was never about the mortgage payment, or about whether they should buy the house. Their real question was "Why do I hate making decisions?" People hate making decisions because limitations equal death.

In Universe One, every decision is a death. If I want to go to movie A, I can't go to movie B. It's a classically constrained universe. But in Universe Two, not only can I see movie A, but on my way out, this guy gives me three free passes to see movie B tomorrow. In one sense, Universe Two is giving and loving. And the idea that the whole universe loves you, even though it sounds corny, is the only force that can conquer Part X.

The person who is good at making decisions is not the one who is "right" most of the time, but the one who works the cycle the most times.

Interpreting intuition is the hardest thing to do because Part X is constantly interfering and co-opting "intuition" to be what it wants it to be. Try to focus on your past history and where you've betrayed yourself, mischaracterized situations, or generally fucked up, and keep your intuition as a sense organ. You do this not because you need to have a model or standard always be right, but to fully sense that you will never go into a situation with enough information. The only thing that matters is the willingness to go forward anyway. The more you do this, the less intimidated you're going to be to take action and the more confidence you will have. Every time you know you're afraid of a consequence, you force yourself forward anyway. It's like putting a penny in the piggy bank—in time, it will become a sought-after experience.

1. **INTUITION**: How we come to trust our instincts.

2. **DECISION**: When we "decide," and cut off other options.

3. **ACTION**: We take action despite having no proof of a certain outcome.

4. **CONSEQUENCES**: This is the most important! Everyone is afraid of consequences. Everyone. This tool offers a way to admit that, but to put it into the training program itself, so that you build a practice of doing an impossible task. This will make it easier when the time comes to make bigger decisions—but it's never going to be easy. When I am working with patients, sometimes they are being cowardly— and sometimes they're simply not ready to handle potential consequences. To prepare yourself to accept larger repercussions, continue to build the muscle by making smaller decisions.

Exercise: Make Decisions

Start in the World of Small Things. You begin at a Chinese restaurant and have thirty seconds to decide what to order. You can't change your mind. As you move throughout your days, find every opportunity to make a decision, even if you don't have enough information—particularly if you don't have enough information—and take the action with speed. Everything you do is to train this organ to tolerate consequences; the point is to not get it "right." As you are working on this process, forget about large decisions like buying a house or quitting your job. The more anxiety you feel, the more you will want to take on smaller and smaller increments of responsibility to build your instinct cycle. And admit that you're not ready—admitting this is a decision in itself.

Patient Story: Porsche Ruined

I was doing a session with someone I knew really well, who was performing as a TV writer well below his talents.

I said to him, "Look, you're an alcoholic. You won't be able to overcome this. You could have a fantastic career as a writer, but not in this condition."

He responded, with complete certainty and looking me right in the eye, "No, I am not an alcoholic. I'm going to tell you about my life, and you'll see that I'm not an alcoholic. You are wrong. You don't know me; I know me."

Three beats passed and then *boom*—we heard a loud *crash*. He had bought a new Porsche that same day, and in that moment, we both knew exactly what had happened. God said, *You schmuck,* and took it away immediately. He was so condescending in his surety that he knew everything about himself—including that he was not an alcoholic—and that he could control everything in his life, then he got a kick in the ass.

Some kid had stolen a car and thought he could outrun the cops, and had smashed into the Porsche. To make things even more dramatic, they towed his Porsche away and left a piece of paper stuck to the ground where his car had been parked—it was a bill for the tow. It was perfect.

If someone thinks that nobody is watching, and that everything that happens is just random—or if someone thinks they know exactly what's supposed to happen—watch out.

Soft Target

A "hard target" in life—an idea about exactly what you want to happen—is not good. A hard target has a bit of a know-it-all-aspect to it, and it lends itself to self-hatred because it has a perfectionistic attitude toward the world. A soft target, on the other hand, leaves room for imperfection. It doesn't say *anything goes,* but it's almost like going into a bar where the target on the wall is bigger. Having a soft target allows you to take a punch and recover more quickly. When you're trying to do something that makes you feel insecure, or if you're not sure you can do it, holding it as a soft target will allow for the process to unfold.

It's a bit like going for a jump shot and thinking, *Oh shit, I hope it goes in.* I bet in that moment, you're stiff. I was playing in a basketball game long ago, and I was way out, about twenty-five feet from the net. The referee put the whistle in his mouth to call a dead ball. I went for the jump shot—I was barely paying attention because the ball was dead. I was incredibly relaxed and the ball swished in. We were killing the other team by thirty points, so it didn't matter anyway, but at sixteen years old, I realized that if I could stay in that state when the ball was *not* dead, I would be unstoppable. I had no idea how to do that practically at that point, but it was a good feeling.

The type of person who holds hard targets—who wants to hear the bells ring, who wants to get a blow job—defines the value of what they're doing by achieving a specific result. That's not a functional way to live. It's the cosmic twins—I want absolute certainty, but by going for the hard target, I end up with absolute terror.

Tool: Salad Dressing

You need two ingredients to make a salad dressing. This is the force that creates everything. It's only potent when it has two ingredients in it—one of the ingredients is material and the other is spiritual. Either one of them alone is impotent. Not only do you have to combine the two at all moments, but the mixture is constantly changing. So if you have a very rigid goal, you are always going to end up fucked-up, because the world is mutable and shifting, and you need to be flexible. Because salad dressing is an endlessly self-adjusting combination of the two opposing forces in the universe, if you're flexible, you have much more agency to respond to what happens, even if you can't determine, dictate, or guarantee what's going to happen. But flexibility gives you agility; you're more prepared.

We experience everything through a very limited lens. The reason for this is because that "thing" in between either you and another person, or you and a situation, is vibratory—and it is a micro model for you and the universe. I call this salad dressing. You can only find your real self if you develop this habit of a soft target. So a soft target says, *I don't really know exactly what the combination of these things should be, but I know whatever it is, two seconds later it will be something different.* This is why people get so anxious. If you have a soft target, and you're a little bit off, it's okay. Because even if you're largely right, you will still need to reconfigure your target.

Again, God only cares about what's going to happen to you. He doesn't care about your accomplishments, or your lack of accomplishments. He just wants you to make salad dressing and to take action.

I encourage patients to use the salad dressing tool when they're nervous or frightened by someone else, or in a situation where the demand from the other person isn't clear and you don't know how to

SALAD DRESSING

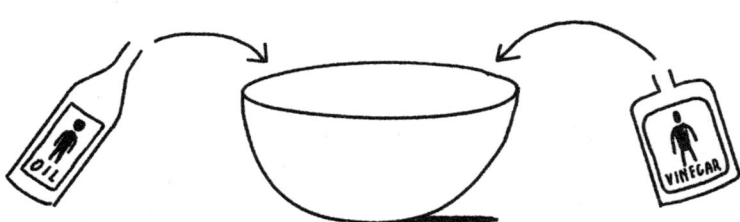

respond. When he turned fifty, one of my patients who is a famous actor finally reached the conclusion that he couldn't predict the quality of a scene, but he knew something else: "At least I've reached the point where I know *something* is going to happen." This is the right attitude.

Tool: Category Three Flow

The definition of flow is the ability to integrate two complete opposites. It's impossible to fully integrate them—but because it's impossible, you get flow. Roy London, the famous acting coach, said that flow feels like nothing. But it's not really nothing; it feels more like ease, or transcendence.

Category Three is like a performance of flow. It's like when you go to buy a car and you're negotiating with a guy—if he can keep the process going, he'll probably win the negotiation. Most people give up because their biases and ego get in the way. Once you lose that back and forth, you lose your power. So the person who can ride with that back and forth and that unpredictability can endure.

Category Three is a version of salad dressing. There are certain situations in which the operation of a process is more important than the details. Aristotle said that affirming two opposites is impossible—what philosophers call "the law of the excluded middle"—but he was wrong. This law asserts that a proposition is only right or wrong, that there's no middle ground. Maybe if you're a bond broker, that holds—but for human beings in general? It destroys them. That state of mind automatically creates two classes, and you can't live like that.

Category Three helps you manage yourself when you have two opposing emotions coming up inside you simultaneously. This is not a theoretical or philosophical concept; it's a physical exercise. It's particularly good for when you're facing a situation where you have a lot of fear or anxiety and are feeling unsettled or in a less evolved state.

Exercise: Entering Flow

Start where there's an imbalance somewhere in your emotional state. Category One is one extreme of this imbalance—let's say you're screaming, you're so upset—and Category Two is its opposite, which is some type of passivity, maybe fear or withdrawal. Close your eyes and feel the rage of Category One without coming up with a reason why. Just feel it. Feel yourself being overly compliant, not speaking up for yourself, overly concerned with what others think of you, etc. Feel that very deeply.

Now go back to the first state, the rage state, and feel that. Then go back to the passive state and feel that. Don't open your eyes. I'm going to tell you to do something, to take action. Don't think. The moment you can absorb what I'm telling you, take the action internally and hit both feelings at the same moment. Although this is impossible, it has the advantage of destroying your ego.

If you practice this exercise enough, you will enter flow, which you can only get by meshing opposites together. Most people don't believe it's even possible, but when you put the two opposites together and maintain the feeling of both simultaneously, you enter flow.

CHAPTER 8

Domain 3: The Need for Constant Work

You Earn: Ability to Access Infinite Forces

The war that we're engaged in is evil versus creativity, and the antidote to evil is to create. Part X's bottom-line goal is to keep you from creating, and from using your Life Force effectively, as the Life Force has real magic (see p. 21). People want superpowers. This is a program to bring out powers or abilities that you already have—and train you to access them continually. Creativity can only thrive when the ultimate value is process, not results.

We live in a universe that is always moving. Everything is constantly changing and shifting—to stay in the flow of the universe, you must be in constant motion, otherwise you lose touch. In fact, higher forces cannot find you if you are not in motion. This need for ceaseless immersion, attention, and commitment takes work— endless work. Forward motion is not possible without momentum generated by the self.

When you can accept that, you start to understand the nature of the universe—and that its infinity means an absence of end points. It is hard for us to understand this, and it makes us depressed, but this is actually an affirmative, existential quality. The three domains represent the face of God: The only way he can reveal himself to you is through a constant, nonstop, no-end-point process that keeps un-folding. You don't reach God; you experience God through this on-going revelation.

Evil is always going to be here. Statesmen, or so-called leaders, insist that evil, or the enemy, will go away and that life will become easy. This is not so. Constant work is necessary so that you can con-tinue to see reality. I always tell patients—especially the ones who have been psychotic—that they've done really well with what's hap-pening, *not* because their psychosis is going to go away, but because it's going to come back anyway. They've done well because of the discipline with which they've attacked it. Even if they say, *No, I had to go to the hospital twice,* it doesn't matter. It only matters if you carry yourself in forward motion. The development of your will, and your commitment not to allow Part X to continue to brainwash you into inaction is a huge win.

Part X will tell you that there's an end point and that success equals that end point. But the whole idea behind the domain of the Need for Constant Work is that the universe is infinite—you have to keep up with the universe, and there is no end point. When you accept constant work and stop avoiding this domain, you are saying, *I accept the fact and am reminding myself of the need to stay connected to infinite, higher forces. I'm going to mimic that ability by staying in motion.*

When you are engaged in infinite creation, you are in Universe Two. When you are convinced that work is finite and you've done enough, you are back in Universe One. It feels as if we've been living in Universe One forever, but not really; this is relatively new. There's a very profound change happening. Even fifty years ago, people had responsibilities that they took more seriously. They were rewarded for accepting responsibility. You might have been a crossing guard, for example, who made sure kids were safe as they went to school. Now, let's say that this crossing guard wins the lottery, and he gets so much money that he can no longer rationalize remaining a crossing guard. The further you go back in time, the less money people had, for one, but there was also less of a conflict between career and money, because a Job with a capital J was what would bring order and meaning to your life. You can't buy that with money. Now, when people get a large amount of money, they can't figure out why they shouldn't quit living. To go back to the Realm of Illusion, when someone like a movie star makes a lot of money, they don't feel any different. Why should they feel different? It's just money. It causes a tremendous leaning toward materialism. What you view as success can give you a lot of stuff, but what it can't give you is what everyone wants, which is a sense of meaning. This can only come when you're in partnership with higher forces.

The material world, Universe One, is a fake world. If you pursue your career and think there's going to be an end point, that you'll get a degree and then a certain job, you're fucked. The material world always betrays you at the end of the day; it prevents you from being what most people would call "successful." Success, like the notion of God, has to be constantly moving because the definition constantly moves. It doesn't matter what happened yesterday; it's an issue of being in a state—a state that has nothing to do with money or competition. You can have a job and take pride in it, or enjoy part of it, but if the money part becomes too big, you have a problem. People believe money is the exonerating factor that will allow them to live on earth without dealing with pain, uncertainty, and the need for constant work.

You must keep doing what's meaningful to you even if you don't have to work anymore. I had five friends who all had a lot of money, and they would play golf and complain about how they couldn't stand the paperwork at the office anymore. All five of them quit or sold their businesses. If I look back to roughly a year or two after they quit, one guy was dead, one guy was in an insane asylum, two of them were not okay, and one of them was fine. It wasn't good odds. They weren't honest with themselves, because all five of them had been taking their identity from their success. This was a mistake, because true success has nothing to do with the metrics of the material world. It has to do with a sense of responsibility within a greater whole. And they had abandoned that. They didn't like the idea that they still had to get up in the morning at six thirty, or watch their diets, or whatever. They thought by getting out of their businesses, they could go on with the way they were living. But without meeting the three requirements of life, the three domains, which are almost the fiber or substance of life—everything fell apart. Even if you meet the fantasy standard of having a lot of money, it can't last—it's not enough. Part X gives you a problem that you don't need to have, like: *I need to have three houses, including two in the Bahamas.* And then it gives you a solution that makes the problem worse. That's what happened to my five friends.

When I tell clients that they need to engage in constant work, they usually tell me they're already burnt out. Burnout comes from seeking some kind of validation or reward in Universe One. You might get what you think is the reward—money, status—but all you're getting is nothing. Because if I finally get a car, or a promotion, or a lollipop, it doesn't matter. Whatever you're getting is not going to give you what the promise is, so you have to keep using your own energy to achieve this. When you are using group energy, or the energy that comes from working with higher forces, it feels limitless, and conversely, endlessly energizing. This type of work gives you energy.

Here's a typical story from my practice: A guy is trying to write a book and he's blocked. He tries this, he tries that, and nothing seems to work. Finally, he's so exhausted, he can't write anymore and he goes to a bar with some friends and they get a little drunk. All of a sudden, the solution comes to him. It's not because he's drunk. The deepest way to think about this type of event is that it has to do with expectations: When he's trying and feels like his expectations will never be met, or that he lacks the ability to meet them in the near-term future, then there's something wrong with him. Meanwhile the creative potential is always there: You have to keep moving forward, without an opinion or expectations, to meet this potential.

You can only access higher forces when you recognize you're engaged in a process and not working toward a singular achievement. In Universe Two, you worship process and view singular achievements as nothing. When you're in a process, the work itself gives you energy. Because the universe keeps moving, the only thing that can be a "success" is a process. You have to have the philosophy where you value the process more than a single attainment.

In life, something will push you to enter the moving world where creative forces live. This "something" could be a lot of things, though it's inherently represented by death. It could be a loss, or it could be a wound. It could be a failure of a business, or it could be a time in third grade when someone punched you in the face. We'll find out what is pushing you there in time. It doesn't matter what it is, just that it had or has the quality of destroying your self-image. It breaks your ego open, in a good way. Nobody accepts this consciously: Nobody wants this. Nobody. As you continue to keep moving forward and outward, the world will ultimately bring you a situation that shatters you altogether.

When I work with someone in the arts, the product or value of their art is totally irrelevant. I don't even want to know what it is. It doesn't matter: All that matters is that they feel in themselves that they're going to have to work for every second of the rest of their life. I tell them that they need to live as though the only thing worth achieving is an inner state that's built on processing—that if they get this, it's the highest gift. That is better than any Academy Award. That's the feeling, or the instinct, or the intuition, that you need to have to be able to perceive infinity. You have to keep going. Whatever your structure is psychologically, it gets torn down every day, and you need to build it back up again. The only way to build it back up is through discipline.

There are three kinds, or levels, of discipline. The first is **reactive**, which is what it sounds like—you are responding to a demand in a disciplined way. This is how you handle a bump in the road, even if it's a big bump. The second is **structural**, which is how you construct your time. This suggests that your day is at least relatively organized and that you show up. And the final kind is **expansive** discipline, which means pushing yourself out into the world in a systematic way, in whatever form this takes. It doesn't matter whether this is working or not. Expansive discipline is the most difficult to use. You must create in an environment where you have no idea whether people are going to accept, or even understand, what you make.

Phil's Story: My Father's Funeral Home

My father had cancer and died suddenly, three or four months after diagnosis. My parents were confirmed atheists, and they wanted to find a way to lay the body to rest without having a religious service. There was a program attached to one of the hospitals in Brooklyn that promised to act fast—if you died, they would move quickly to cremate the body, and make it easy. My father died at three a.m.—he waited until I had left their apartment and driven back to the East Side, which was perfect for him. I drove back and called this service they had lined up. When I opened the door, there was a guy there who looked like Lurch—he was six foot six with a nasty-looking scar, while his colleague looked like a mafioso. He was really grotesque, like someone who would take a bite out of my father's head. I overcame my shocked reaction to this sight and told them the body was in the back. They had a gurney with a black leather body bag, which they whipped out. They had my dad's body in the elevator in under four minutes, at which point I came to.

"Hey, what about the death certificate?" I asked.

"Oh, right." They pulled it out, and I signed it without giving it much thought. As a physician, I'm allowed to sign death certificates. The whole exchange took two minutes, and then they were off. At which point I realized they hadn't known I was a doctor, or asked me for proof. I knew something was wrong and called my father's lawyer, who told me to call the funeral home and tell them I needed the hospital to corroborate that they had in fact received my father's body and cremated it. They were livid and told me that in their fifty years of service to the Brooklyn community, nobody had ever impugned their integrity like this.

The body went where it was supposed to go, I received my proof, and the hoodlums disappeared. The next week, I was walking down the street when I saw the front page of the newspaper: "BODY-SNATCHERS SNATCHED." These guys had been selling bodies on the black market. They had sold this service to my parents as an easy way to do one of life's most difficult tasks. But of course, you cannot avoid the demands of the three domains.

Destroying Your Creations

Creativity is the antidote to evil; Part X wants to keep you in evil; therefore Part X will try to convince you to destroy everything you create.

H.I.P.A.

H.I.P.A. is a model for managing process, made up of four laws: humility, ignorance, poverty, and anonymity. I developed this process originally because the average person in Hollywood has at least a fifty-fifty chance of screwing up their whole career. H.I.P.A. is a way to control your ego so you don't destroy your fate or your own creations. H.I.P.A. is a caretaking tool: It's a way to support and acknowledge that no matter how smart or accomplished you are, that's not enough—the counterforce is coming to try to take you down at any minute. Part X will violate H.I.P.A. to make you think you're using your creative powers properly, when really it's going to make you someone who systematically takes your career apart. Part X tells you that you can create something or have a result and hold onto it. Part X says that you live in a hierarchical world where there are winners and losers. Part X says that you should get all the credit.

H.I.P.A. is the law of the nurturing process, and therefore it's the law of a potent creator, whether you're making a movie, a company, or a family. Every person has a potential, and you are actively working toward realizing that potential. The idea of H.I.P.A. is to protect what you are creating from yourself.

Understanding these principles and referring back to them constantly is the best way to restrain your ego, because if you don't restrain Part X, it will kill you and everything you're actively creating.

HUMILITY: You're not the ruler of the world, no matter how successful or unsuccessful you may be. This law says, *I don't feel as important as I would like to, and I have to accept that.* You may have had big successes and victories, you may be very talented, but there's nothing you can do to lift you above the human condition.

IGNORANCE: I call this law "flying under the banner of igno-rance." It states that neither do I know the true value of what I'm doing, nor is it possible for me to know the future.

POVERTY: This is the hardest law to understand: It states that we can never possess the idea or concept or structure that we're working on. For example, let's say that you work on something until one o'clock in the morning, and then you go to sleep. When you wake up, it's gone. There's nothing there, and you need to start again. If you build a table, it's there the next morning, but if you're build-ing something that's connected to higher forces that has spiritual power, you'll never be able to firmly possess or own it. It's not a con-crete, fixed, or tangible thing. It's an invisible structure that has im-pact, but you just can't see it at work or nail it down.

ANONYMITY: This law states that nobody is really going to know whether you're doing these exercises or not doing them. You don't need to shout to the world that you're making changes—just make the changes and don't lie to yourself. A group of people who have an opinion about who you are in the world, your entourage, your part-ner, your coworkers, may suspect, but at the end of the day, they don't give a shit anyway. That's just the way the universe is. You must do this work without recognition or acknowledgment, because if you don't, you will be looking behind you to see how everyone else perceives your value.

Tool: String of Pearls

We need a functional definition of success in our culture, particu-larly because it's so wrapped up with identity. You can't structure your life around an identity where you win and you're a big shot, or you lose and you're nothing. In my practice, I'd see a writer who would say, "*I thought I was a good writer but I'm shitty. I reread the last thing I wrote, and it sucked.*" My next session would be with a differ-ent screenwriter, who would come in, all pissed off: "*I know that spec screenplay was the best they've read all year, and I don't even get a phone call.*" Neither of these responses—I suck, or I'm the greatest—is

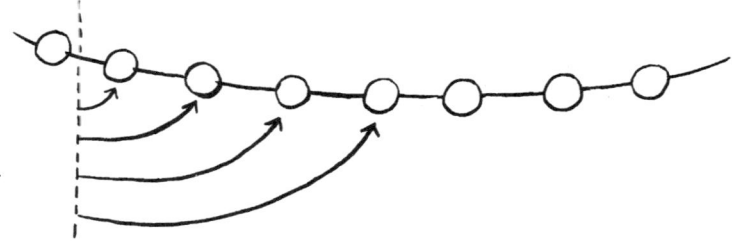

STRING OF PEARLS

within the functional line of creation. Neither of those extremes will help you. You can't ask questions like *Am I succeeding? Am I great or am I failing? Am I worthless?* None of these things are true as an absolute value. The identity you want to have is that you are the person who puts the next pearl on the string. That's it. You're no better, and you're no worse. This is the only way to avoid a common story in our culture, where someone gets to the point where they feel they're so successful, they don't need to try anymore, or the opposite, where they don't believe that anything they do makes a difference. You must return to this idea that you don't know anything, that you're simply putting the next pearl on the string.

When people are working on a project, or working at their jobs, and they hit a glitch, they can choose to say, *Well, this last effort I made was fantastic, and I've proven to everyone that I'm the biggest star in the world,* or they can say the opposite, something like, *I'm a bum and I failed at the key moments.* The person who puts the next pearl on the string says, *I'm neither this guy up here, nor am I the biggest piece of shit; I'm just a schmuck who puts one pearl on the string and then another.* The string of pearls has to do with an identity; it's a tool to be evoked when you're at a crossroads and you're freaking out over the possibility that it won't end in a way that's to your liking. You're building yourself up to the idea that you welcome future events, that you're confident you can handle them because of this tool. In fact, the bigger the event, the better you can handle it. This person doesn't particularly care about the results, because no matter what happens, it's the material world, and it can't be a final step. There's no guarantee of anything actually working, but you are going to proceed anyway. In a world of process, there is no final step. It's an infinite universe, and the best you can do is keep up with the universe through constant work.

Patient Story: A Producer's Bad Review

One day I was doing a session with a big producer who had just had a movie open big. While we were together, he got a call from his office because the writer and director on the film wanted to speak to him. At the time, this writer was so powerful in Hollywood that you couldn't not take his call. So the producer gets on the phone, and the writer is almost crying. He's hysterical. The producer says to him, "You have the number one movie—it broke all records. Why are you upset?" And the writer says, "The guy at the *L.A. Times* gave it a bad review." So the producer asks, "Okay, but how many reviews did you get in total?" And the writer tells him he got thirteen, but one was bad. This bad review ruined his whole day. He was still calling the producer at dinnertime. You want to practice the string of pearls. You're just a guy putting the next pearl on the string.

Tool: Tip of the Spear

The tip of the spear is an illustration of focus—it's a focusing tool. Imagine a traditional spear set against a black background that is really a void. The spear is the only thing that matters. Anything outside of this spear is worthless to us, entirely a distraction. This is an exercise in eliminating everything that pulls your attention. All you want to have left in the tip of the spear are the actions you need to take—you want everything else, whether it's a person or an action, squeezed out. Staying focused takes work. You can think of everything outside of the spear as a classic expression of avoidance. Avoidance is the opposite of being inside of this thing. Part X will throw a thousand distractions at you to get you to step away.

Focus and dimension allow you to build superwill. Focus creates willpower, learning how to focus on an outcome. If the outcome doesn't happen, it doesn't matter. Development of the will is more important than the outcome.

Tool: Plane of Will

Rudolf Steiner says that the only part of you that can pass through to the next level after death is your will. Your will is your higher self, and it's immortal. You cannot activate or be aware of your higher self unless you keep your promises to yourself.

I often tell my patients a story about two pianists. They each go to the same facility at ten o'clock in the morning to practice, and to do whatever a professional pianist would do to prepare. You can't tell the difference between these two guys; everything is the same—same scales, same song. They both leave, but for one of them, it was an almost transcendent experience that gave him a lot of power. The other is unfazed.

The reason the one guy experienced transcendence is that he's pre-committed. At ten o'clock the night before, he knows he'll be in the practice room twelve hours later. He's made a commitment, and he has to keep that commitment. He does this again and again, every day. This is the instinct cycle of commitment, action, commitment, action. Every time he does this, he is activating his higher self, the immortal part of him. People who do this get visited by the gods. An art student once asked Picasso whether he thought inspiration was real in the arts. He said, "Inspiration exists, but it has to find you working." When you make sure that God "finds you working," you set the attitude that will attract other things.

One of my patients was a talented but failing screenwriter, because he would get ideas, and get excited, but he never finished anything. He would just quit. As a result, his confidence started to fail. I explained the plane of will to him, that you must do A today and B tomorrow. You must keep promises to yourself. It doesn't matter how good the work is: The worst finished script is worth more than the best unfinished script. You cannot connect to the underlying structure of creation, you can't harmonize with the universe, if you do not respond to the demand of constant work.

Many of my patients who are writers are excellent at living inside the plane of will—they don't say that they are being more disciplined; they say they are in the plane of will, because it's a place that they can visit and touch.

Exercise: Your Church

You need to think about the plane of will mythologically. What this means is that it doesn't matter what the content or specifics of your goal or plans are. Instead, you must raise your perception to a higher, non-singular level. Your goal can't be the "goal," or end product. Your goal must be the process, to put yourself in the plane of will as part of a journey. Imagine that you're a weight lifter and you have a big meet in a month. If you're serious, and if you're competitive, you're going to start preparing. Every time you work out, you pick up ever-heavier weights. It's not about the weight per se; it's about identifying as a person who lifts heavier and heavier weights. Forget about your goals: Identity is a process. Make this your religion. You don't need to believe in God or higher forces. Just treat this process as divine, and make the plane of will your church.

Phil's Story: The Pigeons

When I lived in New York City, every day I would take a walk through Riverside Park at around three o'clock. There was always an old lady there with a brown paper bag of breadcrumbs that she would throw to the birds. Maybe a hundred or two hundred birds would gather for their meal. It was fine; I was at peace with the pigeons. Then one day, as I walked past the bench, I noticed she wasn't there. But do you know who was there? A zillion fucking pigeons. Believe it or not, this relates to the plane of will. The discipline with which you conduct your everyday business, the systemized way you show up, creates a space. It's not an arbitrary space. Through your work ethic and your habit, you achieve an immediate sense of accomplishment. The pigeons in this case recognize this old lady's cue. People always say, *"When it comes to the plane of will, can't I skip a day?"* Sure. But presenting yourself in a rhythmically predictable way attracts higher forces.

The Y

We've finally arrived at "the Y," when all of these triads and pyramids coalesce into a single symbol. While the Life Force is represented by a vertical pyramid, the Y is a horizontal pyramid, driving you forward, its circular base united by the three domains, represented by harmonizing Willing, Feeling, and Thinking. These three domains are the three different faces of God—they are the unifying trinity. The Y is a picture of both the heart of the entire universe and the innermost soul of every individual. It's both, which is what gives it such power.

There is an inherent contradiction in trying to define the Y for you with any certainty: In reality, I can't. And it won't surprise you to hear that I won't be offering you any proof. What I can offer is that the Y is a mysterious energy system that created the whole universe. Its credential is that it can create out of nothing. It is impossible to even think about what this means. It feels to me like a force that pulls us forward, a force that only turns on when all three domains coalesce into a state of all-inclusive wholeness.

Unlike a binary or twosome, where you are set up in opposition to something else, often in conflict, three has a different energy—an energy that sets everything in motion. This is why our cosmos is full of trinities, whether it's past, present, and future; first person, second

EACH LINE REPRESENTS 1 OF 3 DOMAINS

CIRCLE REPRESENTS FUll INTEGRATION OF 3 DOMAINS

THE "Y" = MAGIC!

person, third person; birth, life, death; beginning, middle, end; etc. Three is a dynamic number—with two, there's no promise that you can move forward or get anywhere. The Y symbol carries with it both personal power and simultaneously a condensation of every power in the universe. The Y is the primal form that this thing takes. You have to put the three things back together again: You don't end up with three times the power; you end up with a thousand times the power. This symbol has movement.

Before Christ and the Trinity, the Hebrews were stuck in a static relationship with God. Christ came and, at least mythologically, split the thing from a rigid two-way relationship into a Trinity. The Christian Trinity actually represents God being willing to share his creative powers with human beings. Before that, human beings didn't share his power. They shared the fruit of his power. It's not the same thing. The Trinity liberated people to create.

We want and need to be part of a group while simultaneously being self-expressive—access to the superpowers we've discussed in this book depend on balancing these two states. In the Middle Ages, they called the balancing element that contained eternal life "the philosopher's stone," but to me it is the Y. It has the ability to harmonize all of these different qualities.

The confluence of the three lines represents the center of the universe, which is also the center of every human being. This symbol brings order to human consciousness, otherwise everything degrades into chaos. This is a symbol of all the lines functioning in harmony with one another, all inclusively. All three are necessary to make a whole. Each domain will bring you to a point at the center of the Y. The Y becomes the end product of human potential. And it doesn't stay still; it needs to be dealt with over and over again.

When the three domains are touching, the result is joy. I'm not talking about happiness; I'm talking about joy, which is a synonym for magic, or the power of creativity. The same force that created the universe is the exact same force that the human being can tap into to create something on their level. Joy is very emotional but out of your control—you can't fabricate joy. Joy is part of your reaction to your trip through the universe, or through your own life. There are certain demands that life will make of you that seem impossible, and you will have no idea how to transact with them, but somehow you learn how to do it. You have relinquished any sense of control and allowed the Life Force to lead.

From this point on, we should think of all the domains, all three of them, as *one*. It is almost like praying to the three parts of them simultaneously. If there's a part you're still avoiding, then you can't connect to the Y. I'm not sure which comes first, the chicken or the egg, but if there's anything you are avoiding in each domain, the Y almost disintegrates, or somehow turns into the enemy. It turns into a block. You can only activate human potential when all three domains are functioning as a whole. Each domain connects you to the middle of the Y, and that gives you a fluid kind of wholeness—a wholeness that is always present, but not always uncovered or realized. It's a bit like how Michelangelo talked about liberating the sculpture from the marble. For him, it was about taking the unnecessary parts away. Similarly, our potential is complete and whole; it's just hard to access. Wholeness doesn't mean that everything in the world is dumped in your lap; it means that nothing is excluded. It has to be considered in terms of its negative energy. As the picture of the Y implies, it's already a whole—we've cut it into pieces, into these three domains, but together they still make a whole. When the Y constellates itself, it activates an infinite and total potential. So when you're looking at the Y, you are almost looking infinitely into the future. It's the ultimate, infinite creative tool.

The kaleidoscope is a useful metaphor, because what it says is that everything is present in the whole—you can rearrange the parts of the kaleidoscope, but you are working with the same totality of potential.

You cannot escape or be exonerated with avoidance. If you want to avoid something in any of these three domains, then the Y, which represents infinite creativity, remains locked. And then you can't access this plane or state. However, if you accept the demands of each of the three domains—which means you're not allowed to avoid anything—then you get real magic, because you're dealing with God as a whole. If you're not connected to all three domains, you don't get these superpowers, because what triggers them is a totalistic wholeness. They mean nothing unless wholeness is achieved. And for things to be whole, they must be inclusive: All three domains must come online for you to access these superpowers in an interactive way—it's not about "winning" in every domain. In fact, the Y only puts you more firmly in the domains, but with superpowers.

The Y gives you access to a heightened perspective of awareness. The Y is like a badge that allows you to go through a portal. It's real and alive. I want to remind you about the two ways we perceive reality. Universe One is a universe that human beings use or adapt as a habitual way of defining reality for themselves, and the way they define it is *there is no value without numerical proof.* Universe Two is totally different and says *value is a functional process that you have to keep working on and working on.* The good news is that it's functional. The whole thing is designed by God. It's not exactly that you are God or that you are just human, but getting into that space where you can combine the two and find the ability to create is foundational to the creativity of Universe Two. And it's not what you created yesterday or in junior high, the value point is: *What are you creating right now?* It's about creativity in the present. Someone might say, "Isn't that limiting?" The answer is no, because you can apply that creativity to anything. The Y is the state that you can reach if you follow these rules. If you're not avoidant, you can reach this state. And once you reach this state, you have the ability to look at life in Universe Two.

Why is a question mark, and the Y is the answer—keep away from *why*. It is run by Part X and it fucks with your brain. Knowing *the why* is a booby prize: You never will. But recognizing and accessing the Y requires accepting that it won't give you certainty, freedom from pain, or exoneration from the need for constant work—that would be the Realm of Illusion, even though you think that by mastering these domains you've transcended them. Realizing the Y puts you even more in the domains. You will still need to contend with pain, uncertainty, and the need for constant work, but you will be doing this in a way that Part X can't stop you.

It gives you a superpower, but you can't achieve it alone. You can't prove these things. My response to the request for proof is to tell clients to act as if it all has meaning, and it will. Real magic is collective magic.

ACKNOWLEDGMENTS

I wrote this book with the intention of breaking new ground in the study of human beings. To the extent I succeeded, it was with the help of an unusual group of people who were more than generous with their support and encouragement. In no particular order: Marisela Jimenez, Aline Garcia, Barry Michels, Jamie Rose, Alicia Wells, Michael Gendler, Leila Tejani, Greg Mollica, Nicholas Blechman, Dennis Ambrose, Ben Greenberg, and Jennifer Joel.

As lucky as I was for the support of these people, there were two others whose presence seemed like more than luck, as if they were placed here by something higher. I am thankful beyond words for your magic: Sarai Jimenez and Elise Loehnen.

PHIL STUTZ graduated Phi Beta Kappa from City College in New York City and received his MD from New York University. He worked as a prison psychiatrist on Rikers Island and then in private practice in New York before moving his practice to Los Angeles in 1982. He is the bestselling co-author of *The Tools, Coming Alive,* and *Lessons for Living.*

ELISE LOEHNEN is the bestselling author of *On Our Best Behavior* and host of the podcast *Pulling the Thread.* She has co-written twelve books, five of which were *New York Times* bestsellers. She was the chief content officer of goop, and she co-hosted *The goop Podcast* and *The goop Lab* on Netflix. Previously, she was the editorial projects director of *Condé Nast Traveler.* Elise lives in Los Angeles with her husband and two sons.

| ABOUT THE TYPE |

This book was set in Garamond, a typeface originally designed by the Parisian type cutter Claude Garamond (c. 1500–61). This version of Garamond was modeled on a 1592 specimen sheet from the Egenolff-Berner foundry, which was produced from types assumed to have been brought to Frankfurt by the punch cutter Jacques Sabon (c. 1520–80).

Claude Garamond's distinguished romans and italics first appeared in *Opera Ciceronis* in 1543–44. The Garamond types are clear, open, and elegant.